Series / Number 07-065

THREE-WAY SCALING AND CLUSTERING

PHIPPS ARABIE
University of Illinois, Urbana

J. DOUGLAS CARROLL
AT&T Bell Laboratories, New Jersey

WAYNE S. DeSARBO
University of Pennsylvania

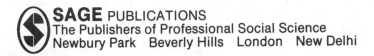

SAGE PUBLICATIONS
The Publishers of Professional Social Science
Newbury Park   Beverly Hills   London   New Delhi

For information address:

SAGE Publications, Inc.
2111 West Hillcrest Drive
Newbury Park, California 91320

SAGE Publications Inc.   SAGE Publications Ltd.
275 South Beverly Drive   28 Banner Street
Beverly Hills   London EC1Y 8QE
California 90212   England

SAGE PUBLICATIONS India Pvt. Ltd.
M-32 Market
Greater Kailash I
New Delhi 110 048 India

International Standard Book Number 0-8039-3068-2

Library of Congress Catalog Card No. 87-061277

FIRST PRINTING

When citing a university paper, please use the proper form. Remember to cite the correct
Sage University Paper series title and include the paper number. One of the following
formats can be adapted (depending on the style manual used):

(1) IVERSEN, GUDMUND R. and NORPOTH, HELMUT (1976) "Analysis of Variance." Sage University Paper series on Quantitative Applications in the Social Sciences,
07-001. Beverly Hills: Sage Pubns.

OR

(2) Iversen, Gudmund R. and Norpoth, Helmut. 1976. *Analysis of Variance.* Sage University Paper series on Quantitative Applications in the Social Sciences, series no. 07-001.
Beverly Hills: Sage Pubns.

CONTENTS

Series Editor's Introduction

Three-Way Scaling and Clustering, by Phipps Arabie, J. Douglas Carroll, and Wayne S. DeSarbo, is a welcome addition to the Quantitative Applications Series. It is written by the most knowledgeable scholars of the topic and it builds nicely on an earlier volume in this series, *Multidimensional Scaling*, by Joseph B. Kruskal and Myron Wish. The Kruskal and Wish volume is an introduction to the concepts and techniques of multidimensional scaling, was written for the novice, and has been quite successful in introducing social scientists to the topic. This volume takes up where the Kruskal and Wish volume leaves off, and assumes a working knowledge of the material covered in the earlier volume and goes well beyond it. Section Four of the Kruskal and Wish volume introduces the topic of the INDSCAL model, and *Three-Way Scaling and Clustering* begins with a review and application of the INDSCAL model.

A second prerequisite for the reader of this volume is a working knowledge of matrix algebra. N. Krishnan Namboodiri's volume in this series, *Matrix Algebra: An Introduction* provides the necessary material. The present monograph is therefore at the intermediate level of difficulty. It is not for the uninitiated because it assumes a previous exposure to topics in multidimensional scaling and a working knowledge of some basic mathematical tools necessary in doing and understanding social science methodology.

Arabie, Carroll, and DeSarbo begin their discussion with an example of the use of the INDSCAL model, they then present the model itself, and finally they return to another extended example. The initial example is the Rosenberg-Kim study of English kinship terms. This approach is very well chosen because the authors have assumed that the reader has already had a brief introduction to the INDSCAL model, at least at the level covered in the Kruskal and Wish volume. As a result, the Rosenberg and Kim example is an excellent mechanism to draw the reader into the discussion quickly and completely. Then the presentation of the model and concepts grows nicely from within a context that has been set by the authors. A second example firms up the reader's understanding of the model.

After they cover the INDSCAL model, the authors present a detailed analysis of SINDSCAL and provide an introduction to other three-way scaling models as well as individual differences *clustering* models. The Rosenberg and Kim data are used again to illustrate the

6

INDCLUS clustering model. The authors thoughtfully include a series of appendices providing readers with the control cards to analyze one of the examples using SINDSCAL, and discussing several procedures for fitting the INDSCAL model.

This monograph, then, provides a sophisticated overview and analysis of three-way scaling procedures. It should prove most helpful to researchers in psychology, marketing, and educational psychology; and it will also be useful to a number of scholars in sociology and political science who study public opinion or who engage in various forms of roll-call analysis in legislative or judicial bodies of government. We are delighted to add it to our list of publications in the *Quantitative Applications Series*.

—John L. Sullivan
Series Co-Editor

ACKNOWLEDGMENTS

For comments on earlier versions of this paper, the authors would like to thank J. P. Cunningham, Y. Dural, K. Faust, L. E. Jones, M. Keefe, J. B. Kruskal, F. Lundström, S. Pruzansky, S. D. Soli, M. Wish, and especially J. Daws. Encouragement from the Editors and the staff at Sage Publications has been beneficial. The first author's participation in writing this paper was supported by AT&T Information Systems through the Industrial Affiliates Program of the University of Illinois. We would also like to thank Lynn Bilger, Martina Bose, Rhoda Iosso, and Tom Sharpe for superb technical assistance.

THREE-WAY MULTIDIMENSIONAL SCALING AND RELATED TECHNIQUES

PHIPPS ARABIE
University of Illinois at Champaign

J. DOUGLAS CARROLL
AT&T Bell Laboratories
Murray Hill, New Jersey

WAYNE S. DeSARBO
Wharton School
University of Pennsylvania

1. INTRODUCTION

Kruskal and Wish (1978) provide a detailed introduction to the use of multidimensional scaling (MDS), with emphasis on situations where the data analyst has a single input (proximities) matrix. That is, one has a matrix whose entries consistently gauge the similarity (or dissimilarity — more generally, proximity) between all pairs of a set of objects. (By "objects," we mean stimuli, political candidates, biological entities, variables, or whatever other objects the user seeks to position in a spatial representation. In Kruskal and Wish's [1978, pp. 7-9] first application of MDS, the "objects" are cities, and the "spatial representation" consists of points, corresponding to the cities, in a plane.)

This single input proximity matrix contains for each pair of objects one entry designating the similarity/dissimilarity between the pair. These entries may have come from a single subject or other source of data, or have been aggregated over sources of data. In the former case, one is explicitly declaring interest only in the data from an individual source. For aggregated data, one is implicitly assuming a set of subjects (or other sources of data) homogeneous with respect to generating their data. Tucker and Messick (1963) were the first to address the problem of spatially representing a set of matrices from heterogeneous sources for which an overall analysis was sought. In attempting to strike a balance between an analysis using data aggregated over all sources (thus suppressing all differences among conditions) versus a separate analysis for each data matrix (thus rendering the analyses difficult to compare and producing a potential surplus of detail), Tucker and Messick (1963) devised a "points-of-view" approach that we view as seeking to "cluster" or partition the data matrices into relatively homogeneous subgroups, aggregate within, and then run an analysis for each such subgroup. (This approach in several variants was based on a factor or components analysis of correlations, covariances, or cross-products of entries in these data matrices.) Thus began the tradition of analyzing "three-way" data matrices.

In the present paper, we wish to discuss methods for three-way approaches to MDS and related techniques. We shall emphasize work for which publications are widely available giving explicit details of models, algorithms, and software. The techniques covered in the present paper are limited to those which follow the more recent strategy of conducting one overall analysis, yielding a "group" solution, but with models also providing variation in parameters corresponding to individual sources of data. For example, Carroll and J. J. Chang's (1970) INDSCAL (for INdividual Differences SCALing) model assumes the objects are embedded in a continuous space common to all sources of data, while portraying individual differences among sources of data by differentially shrinking or stretching (viz., weighting) each dimension in the spatial solution according to the implied emphasis given to the dimension by a specific source of data. The Carroll and Arabie (1983) INDCLUS (for INdividual Difference CLUStering) model represents the structure of the set of objects as a set of discrete, possibly overlapping clusters common to all sources of data. Whereas the INDSCAL model provides differential weighting of *dimensions* over individual sources of data, the INDCLUS model portrays individual differences by weighting *clusters* differentially over individual sources of data.

TERMINOLOGY

Because we believe that the SINDSCAL computer program (Pruzansky, 1975) is the one most commonly used for three-way MDS, we will be emphasizing various aspects of using that program, although other programs will also be considered. To describe the different types of data and models discussed here — and even to explain the title of this paper — it is necessary to introduce some terminology from Carroll and Arabie's (1980) taxonomy of data and models for multidimensional scaling. (Readers interested in a full-length treatment of the typology should consult the 1980 article, as well as Stevens, 1951, Coombs, 1964, Tucker, 1964, Shepard, 1972a, and de Leeuw and Heiser, 1982. Readers already familiar with standard descriptions of input data for MDS may wish to skip to the next section.)

Following the notation of Kruskal and Wish (1978, p. 16-19), a single (symmetric) *proximity matrix* $\Delta \equiv \{\delta_{ij}\}$ will be assumed to have I rows and I columns indexing the same set of I objects that are in the same order for both rows and columns. (The sign $\equiv$ is read "equals by definition.") Typical measures of proximity include "direct" subjective values of judged similarity, dissimilarity, affinity, substitutability or co-occurrence; "direct" measures based on observation of overt confusion, association or disjunctive reaction time; or "indirect" or "profile" measures derived from the computation of overlap, correlation, or distance between all pairs of objects. (See Coxon, 1982, Ch. 2 for a general discussion.) Entry δ_{ij} in Δ represents the input data value gauging proximity between objects i and j, where i and j both range from 1 to I. We label the single matrix Δ as *two-way* since it has both rows and columns for its two "ways." Thus, we generally refer to an MDS analysis (as covered in Chapters 1-3 of Kruskal and Wish, 1978) involving only one input matrix as a two-way analysis. Because both ways correspond to the same set of objects, we say that only one *mode* (Tucker, 1964) is involved. Thus, the MDS analysis of a single input proximity matrix is said to involve one-mode two-way data (cf. Carroll and Arabie, 1980).

Throughout this paper we will generally assume that the proximity matrix Δ (or a series of them) contains entries that are *symmetric* about the main diagonal; that is $\delta_{ij} = \delta_{ji}$ for $i, j = 1 \cdots I$. When the raw data satisfy this requirement, it is only necessary to read in a lower halfmatrix (or series of them) δ_{ij} ($i = 2 \cdots N$; $j = 1 \cdots i-1$), since the upper triangular matrix would only contain redundant information. The discussion in this paper will generally assume that there are no missing data in the lower triangular halfmatrix. The self-proximity values δ_i contained in the principal diagonal of Δ are not used by most of the programs emphasized in this paper and are thus not usually read in as data.

If the raw data are *not* one-mode (e.g., a two-mode two-way matrix of I objects by S attributes), then pre-processing is required to convert the data to one-mode two-way. Kruskal and Wish (1978, pp. 70-73) consider this situation and provide detailed instructions that will not be repeated here (also see Cronbach and Gleser, 1953, and Carroll, 1968). When the raw data *are* one-mode two-way, as required for the models and programs described here, but are *not* symmetric, two approaches are available. The first uses one of various approaches to "symmetrize" each of the pairs of unequal conjugate values δ_{ij} and δ_{ji} by some type of averaging, to provide a single value (see the Appendix of Arabie and Soli, 1982) which is then entered in a triangular lower halfmatrix. The second and less frequently employed approach is to use one or more of the procedures (e.g., TUCKALS2 of Kroonenberg and de Leeuw, 1980; DeSarbo and Rao, 1984; DeSarbo and Carroll, 1985) that offer an explicit facility for depicting both the row and the column representations of an object being scaled (e.g., both the stimulus and the response for such ostensibly nonsymmetric confusions data as those analyzed below, from Miller and Nicely, 1955).

Kruskal and Wish (1978, pp. 76-78) provide a discussion of metric versus nonmetric approaches to MDS, with the former corresponding to interval and ratio scale data, and the latter to ordinal scale data. For two-way MDS these distinctions have proved quite valuable, but they seem empirically less so for three-way MDS. The present discussion will emphasize metric approaches that assume interval or ratio scale data and use least squares procedures as part of the algorithm for fitting the models to such data, and generally employ variance accounted for as the measure of goodness-of-fit. In practice, however, many applications involving admittedly ordinal data have yielded acceptable goodness-of-fit and plausible substantive interpretations.

Thus far, almost everything said in this section is as relevant to two-way data for MDS as for three-way data. We now turn to the latter and more general case, in which we have a series of $k = 1 \cdots K$ symmetric proximity matrices Δ_k, one from each of K subjects or other sources of data. The left panel of Figure 1 shows such a three-way proximity matrix having square or "full" (two-way) constituent matrices. Because of symmetry, however, the form with triangular lower halfmatrices, given in the right panel of Figure 1, is more commonly used. An entry of proximity within one of these matrices will be denoted as $\delta_{ij,k}$, indicating the proximity between objects i and j, according to the k-th source of data. Recall that each of the K proximity matrices is one-mode two-way. The addition of an extra mode (viz., the *sources* of the K matrices) yields an input data set that is two-mode and three-way. The two modes are objects and sources; the three ways are objects × objects × sources, with corresponding dimensions $I \times I \times K$.

In describing types of data matrices, we need to distinguish between two possible forms of "conditionality." For *one*-mode two-way data, a particular type of data often relevant to MDS (e.g., Green and Rao, 1972, Ch. 1) are row (or column) conditional, in the terminology of Coombs (1964). That is, the meaning of the value of a datum is dependent or conditional upon the row (or column) in which it is

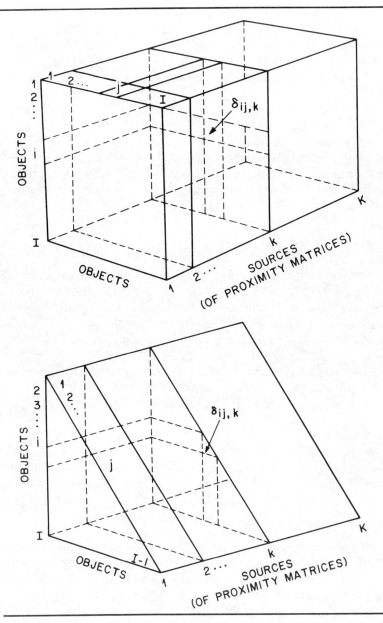

Figure 1: Full matrix (upper panel) and lower triangular matrix (lower panel) input for three-way MDS and related methods. Subscripts *i* and *j* denote objects ($i, j = 1 \cdots I$) and *k* denotes sources ($k = 1 \cdots K$). The right panel assumes that conjugate off-diagonal entries in the full matrix are equal and that self-proximities will not be read. (Modified from Carroll and Wish, 1974a, p. 60.)

located, and data entries are comparable *within* a row (column) but not *between* rows (columns). For two-mode three-way data, Takane, Young, and de Leeuw (1977) introduced the important distinction of *matrix* conditional data, for which entries are comparable within a matrix (i.e., across as well as within rows and columns), but *not* between matrices. A data set whose entries are comparable across matrices is said to comprise matrix *unconditional* data. In contrast, if data from one source were measured in different units or on a different numerical scale from that found in other sources, such data would probably be declared matrix *conditional*. Although situations often arise where data are not as easily classified as the matrix conditional versus unconditional dichotomy might suggest, the distinction can have important implications for how the data are processed by the computer programs discussed below.

2. ILLUSTRATIVE APPLICATION OF INDSCAL

Aside from the Tucker and Messick (1963) approach mentioned earlier, the INDSCAL model of Carroll and Chang (1970) marked a departure for models of three-way MDS. (An overview of other early contributions to this area is given by Carroll and Chang, 1970, pp. 299-313, and of more recent work is given by Carroll and Arabie, 1980, pp. 630-635.) The first *algorithm* and associated computer program for fitting this model was also called INDSCAL (Chang and Carroll, 1969). (The model, without any software for fitting it, was independently proposed by Horan [1969]. An algorithm for fitting the same model was given in an unpublished paper by Bloxom [1968], but was not generally adopted.) Pruzansky (1975) updated the INDSCAL program, and her streamlined version, called SINDSCAL (for Symmetric INDSCAL), will be the program for three-way two-mode scaling emphasized in this paper. (Kruskal and Wish, 1978, provide an introductory discussion of the INDSCAL approach to three-way MDS.)

DESIGN OF ROSENBERG AND KIM'S (1975) EXPERIMENT

In this section of the paper, we give an overview of a data analysis (which used the early INDSCAL program) published by Rosenberg and M. P. Kim (1975), to acquaint readers with the INDSCAL approach to multidimensional scaling. Following this discussion, the next chapter will present the INDSCAL model in greater technical detail and will provide a lengthier presentation of a second published example using the SINDSCAL program (Pruzansky, 1975).

The *objects* of the Rosenberg-Kim study were the 15 kinship terms occurring most commonly in English: aunt, brother, cousin, daughter, father, granddaughter, grandfather, grandmother, grandson, mother, nephew, niece, sister, son, uncle. Note that there are two obvious bases of organization: (a) by generation (from grandparents to grandchildren), and (b) by sex, since all terms except cousin have definite gender in English. Given two conflicting bases for organization, it is naturally of interest to look at differences among groups of subjects in the use of these two schemes of classification, and to see which experimental paradigms and methods for portraying structures in the data could faithfully depict such differences.

The *sources* of data in the Rosenberg-Kim study were $K = 6$ mutually exclusive groups of college students, each of whom received a set of 15 slips of paper, each containing one of the kinship terms. The paradigm for data collection was a "sorting" task, in which a subject is asked to produce a partition of the $(I = 15)$ objects, on the basis of perceived psychological similarity. (For further details on the method of sorting, see G. A. Miller, 1969, and Rosenberg, 1977, 1982.) Eighty-five male and eighty-five female subjects were run in the condition where subjects gave (only) a single-sort of the terms. A different group of subjects (eighty males and eighty females) was told in advance that after making their first sort, they would be asked to give additional subjective partitionings of these stimuli using "a different basis of meaning each time." Rosenberg and Kim used only the data from the first and second sortings for these groups of subjects. Thus, we have the $K = 6$ conditions as our sources for an INDSCAL analysis: females' single-sort, males' single-sort, females' first-sort, males' first-sort, females' second-sort, males' second-sort.

Note that the sources in this analysis are experimental conditions and that data have been aggregated over subjects within each of the six conditions. We emphasize this fact because descriptions (e.g., Carroll and Chang, 1970; Carroll and Wish, 1974a) of the mode differentiating three-way two-mode from two-way one-mode scaling have traditionally labeled the additional mode as "subjects." We prefer the more general designation of "sources" (of data) to include such situations as the present analysis.

THE DATA

Each subject's data can be coded as a symmetric 15×15 binary (0,1) co-occurrence matrix in which a one indicates that kinship terms of the corresponding row and column were sorted into the same group by the subject. The resulting co-occurrence matrices are then summed within each condition to yield an aggregate matrix. At this point, several options can be considered for pre-processing the data, as well as treating each of the six matrices as a similarity matrix and proceeding immediately with the analysis. (The six matrices, converted to dissimilarities by subtracting each entry from the number of subjects in the respective conditions, are listed below in Table 6.) Rosenberg and Kim (1975, p. 492) give details of the pre-processing they used; other discussions can be found in the references cited above for the method of sorting as well as in Carroll and Arabie (1983, pp. 163-164) and references cited there.

INTERPRETATION OF THE RESULTS

As we noted earlier, in this first example of an INDSCAL analysis, we wish to emphasize the substantive interpretation more than the technical aspects of the model and output from the program used to fit it. In the example considered in the next section, this emphasis will be reversed.

Rosenberg and Kim (1975, p. 493) used the INDSCAL program (Chang and Carroll, 1969) to seek spatial representations of the objects (kinship terms) and, separately, of the sources (conditions) in four, three, two, and one dimensions. Then, using criteria discussed below and emphasizing interpretability, the authors opted to use the three-dimensional solution. Figure 2 reproduces this spatial solution for the kinship terms. (The points representing these terms have been placed on rods to convey depth in the third dimension.) Such a solution is traditionally called the *group space* or "stimulus space" although neither term successfully conveys the fact that it is a space of objects that is characteristic of the entire group of K distinct conditions.

Note that the orientation of the axes in Figure 2 is given by the output (described below) from the INDSCAL program, without any need of follow-up analysis to find a rotation, as usually required by factor analysis. This uniqueness of orientation of the group space's solution must be qualified in three details. First, the axes may be reflected, so that, for example, the "poles" used in Figure 2 could, with equal mathematical legitimacy, be inverted so that left and right positions would be reversed for the second dimension, or up and down reversed for the third dimension, etc. These spatial transformations correspond, of course, to mirror reflections.

Second, again with equal mathematical legitimacy, the axes and their corresponding weights can be permuted (i.e., interchanged). For example, the dimension currently labeled as "1" could be rotated to the position currently held by "3", so that the two axes would be interchanged. These permutations and reflections can be viewed as rotations through angles that are multiples of 90°. (Although the preceding sentence is not quite technically correct for reflection of an odd number of dimensions, we believe that statement will suffice for this paper.) It is important to note, however, that rotations through an

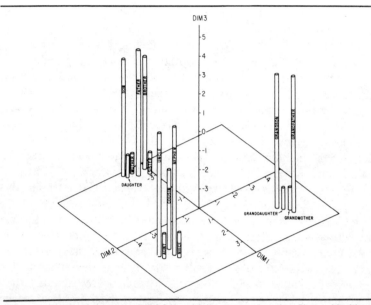

Figure 2: Three-dimensional INDSCAL object space for the fifteen kinship terms studied by Rosenberg and Kim. (Reproduced with permission from Rosenberg and Kim, 1975, p. 493.)

arbitrary angle are not permitted. Another way of summarizing the admissible transformations is that although the axes have an inherently fixed or preferred orientation, the data analyst — as observer of the spatial solution — is not limited to any particular viewing angle (cf. Shepard and Arabie, 1979, p. 116; Asimov, 1985) and can thus choose a convenient vantage point that may correspond to a reflection or permutation of the orientation in which the axes emerge in numerical or plotted form from a computer program fitting the INDSCAL model. (This issue will be considered in more technical detail below.)

Third, certain patterns can arise in the data so that certain subsets of the dimensions in an INDSCAL space are not uniquely determined. In the solution presented in Figure 2, Rosenberg and Kim (1975, p. 494) noted that the dimensions labeled "1" and "2" in Figure 2 are not uniquely oriented vis-à-vis each other (but the plane they form is uniquely oriented vis-à-vis Dimension 3) and are thus properly interpreted as a plane rather than as separate dimensions. (The evidence of this nonunique orientation is given in Pruzansky's [1975] SINDSCAL program by the "normalized sum of products" for subjects [i.e., sources] and will be discussed below.)

With these caveats on the uniqueness of the axes of the object space now given, we turn to the substantive interpretation of Figure 2.

Dimension 3 is immediately interpretable as gender, with the male kin terms toward the top, female terms toward the bottom, and cousin in an appropriately intermediate location. For the plane formed by Dimensions 1 and 2, three ostensible groups are apparent: grandparents and grandchildren, nuclear family (mother, father, sister, brother, daughter, son), and "collaterals" (aunt, uncle, cousin, niece, nephew). Although it may be tempting to refer to three "clusters," to do so would not be appropriate. Demonstrating that clusters are indeed present requires using a method designed to find clusters, rather than using a scaling, factor analytic, or other explicitly spatial model. Rosenberg and Kim used hierarchical clustering (see Hubert, 1974; Hartigan, 1975) to seek clusters, and we will use INDCLUS later in this monograph on these same data.

In addition to comparing the spatial representation of the kinship terms with various theoretical positions taken by anthropologists, Rosenberg and Kim (1975, p. 494) also presented the INDSCAL weights, reproduced here as Table 1, indicating the salience (or importance) attributed to each dimension by each source of data, when the INDSCAL model (presented in the next section) is fitted to the data from the six experimental conditions. As Rosenberg and Kim noted, Dimensions 1 and 2 (interpreted above as a plane) were weighted much more heavily by the two groups in the single-sort condition than in the four multiple-sort conditions. Subjects in those latter four conditions gave much greater salience to (i.e., had larger weights for) Dimension 3, interpreted earlier as gender, than to the first two dimensions. These differences in the patterns of the weights over the different sources of data are the basis of the preferred orientation conferred by fitting the INDSCAL model. That is, an arbitrary change in the orientation of the axes would result in different values fitted for the weights of the rotated axes and thus a reduction in goodness-of-fit. Note how little the weights vary for the first two dimensions over the different sources. Because the weights differ so little over the two dimensions, a rotation of the solution along the plane formed by Dimensions 1 and 2 would shift the values of the weights (described below in detail) very little, and thus have little effect on the variance accounted for that is being maximized as a measure of goodness-of-fit. Although there are more direct indicators of indeterminate orientation, the parallelism of weights' values across these two dimensions is intuitively connected more directly with the problem. This parallelism is a special case of the more general condition under which orientation is indeterminate within a plane of the object space, namely when the weights for the two corresponding dimensions have a fixed ratio over all sources of data.

TABLE 1

INDSCAL Source Weights for Each of Rosenberg and
Kim's (1975) Experimental Conditions

Group	Dimension		
	1	2	3
Male Respondents:			
Single Sort	.54	.57	.25
Multiple Sort One	.34	.40	.75
Multiple Sort Two	.30	.22	.83
Female Respondents:			
Single Sort	.62	.60	.05
Multiple Sort One	.10	.10	.97
Multiple Sort Two	.47	.46	.53

3. THE INDSCAL MODEL

For each input data value $\delta_{ij,k}$ there is a corresponding reconstructed or estimated distance $d_{ij,k}$ in the matrix $\mathbf{D} \equiv \{d_{ij,k}\}$, indicating the distance between objects i and j in a group object space that has been altered by applying dimension weights (as listed in Table 1 from the Rosenberg and Kim analysis) for source k to stretch and shrink axes differentially. Supplying a specific relationship between the input data values of $\delta_{ij,k}$ and corresponding output values of $d_{ij,k}$ requires several pages of formulae. Relegating such a detailed technical presentation to Appendix B, we begin by noting that the relationship between the two variables is linear for each source of data. Formally,

$$F_k(\delta_{ij,k}) \cong d_{ij,k};$$ [1]

that is, linear functions F_k are fitted between input proximity data values $\delta_{ij,k}$ and corresponding output distances $d_{ij,k}$ for each of the $k = 1 \cdots K$ sources of proximity matrices. (The $\cong$ sign should be read "is approximated by.") Although there is no straightforward single formula relating these two sets of input and output variables, the relationship between the recovered distances $d_{ij,k}$ and the object coordinates (as used to obtain the type of the plot shown in Figure 2) and dimension weights (as listed in Table 1) is easily stated:

$$d_{ij,k} = \sqrt{\sum_{r=1}^{R} w_{kr}(x_{ir} - x_{jr})^2}.$$ [2]

In the formula, w_{kr} is the weight indicating salience or importance of dimension r (where $r = 1 \cdots R$) for source k (where $k = 1 \cdots K$) of proximity data, and x_{ir} and x_{jr} are the respective coordinates of objects i and j along the r-th dimension in the R-dimensional INDSCAL object space.

Several comments are in order concerning matrices $W \equiv \{w_{kr}\}$ and $X \equiv \{x_{ir}\}$, which are both estimated simultaneously (by methods to be explained below) to the input Δ matrix. First, note that the coordinate values in X were used to position the objects in Figure 2. Although no corresponding plot based on W was presented, several will be later. As is apparent in Figure 3, both matrices W and X have the same dimensionality R ($= 3$ in the Rosenberg and Kim solution reproduced earlier), but the continuous spatial representations they offer (of sources or objects, respectively) are in separate spaces. Therefore, the points (weights) representing conditions and those representing objects can *not* be plotted together in a common space.

Unlike the object coordinates x_{ir} which assume both negative and positive values, the weights w_{kr} will generally be nonnegative, even though there is no explicit constraint in the SINDSCAL program (Pruzansky, 1975) forcing them to be greater than or equal to zero. Empirically, it is not unusual to encounter a few slightly negative weights (e.g., $-.04$ to $-.01$) in using the SINDSCAL program, and these are generally viewed as not being appreciably different from zero. The problem, of course, with negative weights having a larger absolute value is that they have no substantive interpretation.

Consider the case in equation [2] when all weights are unitary, i.e., when $w_{kr} \equiv 1.0$. With this stipulation, one has the "unweighted" Euclidean formula for the distance between objects i and j in an R-dimensional space:

$$d_{ij} = \sqrt{\sum_{r=1}^{R} (x_{ir} - x_{jr})^2} \qquad [3]$$

(cf. Kruskal and Wish, 1978, p. 19). Thus, it is the introduction of differentially-valued weights w_{kr} that distinguishes the distance model underlying three-way scaling à la INDSCAL (equation [2]) from two-way scaling (equation [3]) as covered in Kruskal and Wish (1978). (Recall the discussion above where we noted that, because the pattern of weights was so similar across Dimensions 1 and 2 of Rosenberg and Kim's INDSCAL object space, those two dimensions had no preferred orientation and were best interpreted as a plane. Stated differently, those two dimensions were not fitted better by the weighted than by the unweighted version of the model, and had an orientation no more unique than if they had arisen from a two-way MDS analysis, for

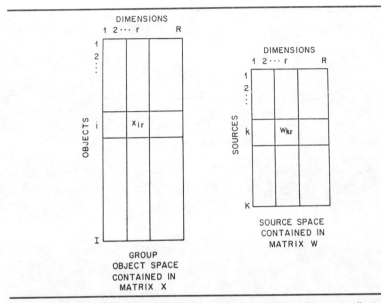

Figure 3: Output matrices **X** and **W**, corresponding respectively to coordinates for objects and sources, resulting from fitting the INDSCAL model. (Modified from Carroll and Wish, 1974a, p. 60.)

which there is, of course, no inherently preferred orientation.) Because of this difference between the types of distance functions assumed, the INDSCAL model is sometimes referred to as the *weighted Euclidean model*. (A generalization of the model to include non-Euclidean distances and corresponding software has been provided by Okada and Imaizumi, 1980, 1986.)

A more geometric interpretation of the role of weights in the INDSCAL model, using artificial data is given in Figure 4 (taken from Carroll and Wish, 1974a). The two-dimensional group object space in the upper left panel of this Figure shows nine objects, labeled A through I, in a lattice configuration, based on the **X** matrix of object coordinates. In the upper right panel, the **W** matrix of weights, which was only listed for the Rosenberg and Kim data in Table 1, has now been realized as a set of coordinates for nine hypothetical sources, whose two-dimensional positions are indicated by the Arabic numerals. Note that all sources are positioned in the positive quadrant (more generally, the positive orthant) or on segments of the axes defining it. It should also be added that the particular choice of $I = 9$ objects and $K = 9$ sources for this artificial example is entirely arbitrary and was selected merely for graphic purposes. (As is intuitively obvious from comparing equations [2] and [3], there must be at least $K = 2$ sources

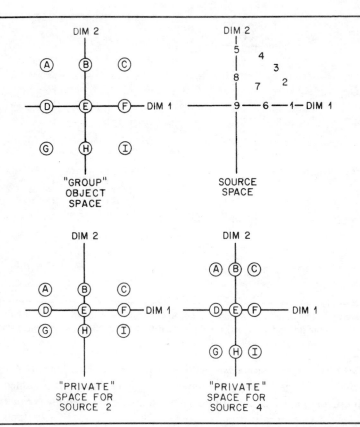

Figure 4: Hypothetical example illustrating the INDSCAL model. Weights from the source space are applied to the dimensions of the "group" object space to produce "private" spaces for sources 2 and 4. Although technically the square roots of the weights are applied to the dimensions, in this demonstration, the first power of the weights has been used to accentuate the effects of differential weighting. (Modified from Carroll and Wish, 1974a, p. 62.)

of proximity matrices in a SINDSCAL analysis, as a necessary but not always sufficient condition for obtaining a uniquely preferred orientation of the axes in the object space.)

Numerically, the weights w_{kr}, as given in the output from SINDSCAL or some other programs for fitting the INDSCAL model, gauge the judgmental or perceptual salience of dimension r for the k-th source of data. In this text, we will sometimes refer to the weights as "dimension weights" and at other times as "source weights." Since the weights are jointly determined *both* by the sources of proximity data *and* the dimensions (i.e., w_{kr} is the weight for source k on dimension r), we trust that the reader will regard these two different ways of referring to the weights as synonymous.

So long as the weights are positive, they can be regarded graphically as stretching factors applied to the dimensions of the "group" object space. Thus, these differential weights produce for each source of proximity data a "private" object space by rescaling (differentially stretching and shrinking by a factor given by the *square root* of the respective weights) the dimensions of the group object space. In Figure 4, for example, the weights fitted for source 3 are equal along the two dimensions. (For an analysis of real data, these weights would be given as output from a program for fitting the INDSCAL model.) This source's "private" object space would look much like the group object space, except for an overall rescaling factor applied uniformly to both dimensions, and thus leaving their relative importance or saliences unchanged. The private object spaces for sources 2 and 4 are shown in the left and right lower corners, respectively, of Figure 4. Source 2, with greater weight for Dimension 1 than for 2, has a private perceptual space that is compressed along the axis of Dimension 2, or, equivalently, stretched along Dimension 1. This situation is reversed for source 4, whose estimated weight is higher on the second dimension than on the first.

INHERENTLY UNIQUE ORIENTATION OF AN INDSCAL OBJECT SPACE

We noted earlier that an important benefit of fitting the INDSCAL model is the inherently unique orientation that usually results for the object space, in contrast to the rotationally invariant solutions from two-way Euclidean MDS. Substantively, this uniqueness suggests that the dimensions of an INDSCAL object space should correspond to "fundamental" perceptual or judgmental — different terms may be appropriate for disciplines other than psychology — processes whose importance, strength, or salience may differ from source to source (e.g., over subjects or experimental conditions). Mathematically, a rotation or other arbitrary transformation (other than a reflection or permutation of axes, as discussed above) will change the family of admissible transformations of a group object space, and thus the family of matrices (i.e., patterns of weights) for individual sources. As a demonstration using the artificial example in Figure 4, note that a 45° rotation of the group object space would change the family of "private" object spaces from the present collection of rectangular lattices to one of differently shaped rhombi, differentially stretched or shrunk as shown in Figure 5.

A further inspection of equation [2], which is reproduced here for the reader's convenience, will demonstrate why reflections and permutations of the axes in the object space leave the interobject distances **D** (and thus the goodness-of-fit) unchanged:

$$d_{ij,k} = \sqrt{\sum_{r=1}^{R} w_{kr}(x_{ir} - x_{jr})^2} \; .$$

A reflection of r-th axis of the object space simply effects the transformation $x'_{ir} = -x_{ir}$ where the object coordinates resulting from the reflections are designated by a prime sign (i.e., apostrophe). Thus, a reflection of the r-th axis replaces $(x_{ir} - x_{jr})^2$ in the immediately preceding formula with $(x'_{ir} - x'_{jr})^2$ which in turn is equal to the expression originally found in equation [2], as reproduced above. Similarly, if we add an arbitrary constant c_r to each of the object coordinates x_{ir} and x_{jr} and thus effect a change of origin (or "translation") for the r-th axis, this constant will vanish when $([x_{ir} + c_r] - [x_{jr} + c_r])^2$ is computed. For a permutation of the axes, the demonstration is even simpler. This transformation simply interchanges axes r and r' (where r and r' are both of the range $1 \cdots R$). Thus, in equation [2], x_{ir} and x_{jr} are simply interchanged with x'_{ir} and x'_{jr} respectively. The net effect of a permutation of axes is thus simply to change the order in which numbers enter the summation in equation [2]. That is, although the subscripts (and order of summation) are affected by a permutation of axes, neither the numerical values of the arguments of this equation nor the resulting interobject distances are changed. *In summary, neither translation, reflection, nor permutation of axes in an INDSCAL object space has any statistical or substantive importance when solutions are interpreted.*

Further inspection of equation [2] for reconstructed interobject distances yields another observation relevant to the object space: If the objects' coordinates (x_{ir} and x_{jr}) are multiplied by any arbitrary (nonzero) constant, the change can be compensated for by multiplying the weights (w_{kr}) by the reciprocal of the square of that constant, so that the distances on the left side of equation [2] remain unchanged. Thus, one could arbitrarily "scale" the coordinates (and, thus, the corresponding dimensions) of the *object* space and compensate by rescaling the weights that constitute the coordinates of the *source* space. (In more technical terms, we say that there is an "identification" problem of the **X** and **W** parameters when one fits the INDSCAL model.)

Carroll and Chang's (1970, p. 289) approach to this problem was to "normalize" the object space so that along each of the R dimensions taken separately, the sum of the squared coordinates totals one. (In addition, the sum of the coordinates along each dimension is zero, so

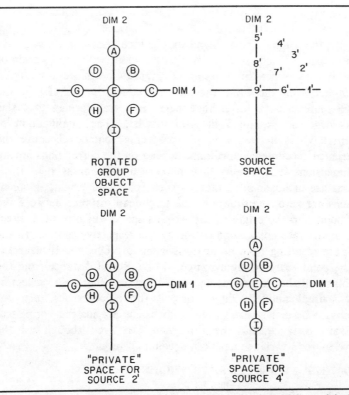

Figure 5: Effects of rotation of group object space on INDSCAL model. Note that private spaces for sources 2′ and 4′ (having the same pattern of weights as sources 2 and 4 in Figure 4, but not to be regarded respectively as identical sources) are differently shaped rhombi rather than differently shaped rectangles as in Figure 4. Finally, note that *no* pattern of weights in the source space, when applied to the rotated group object space in Figure 5, will produce either of the rank orders of distances resulting for sources 2 and 4 in Figure 4 (while, conversely, no pattern of source weights applied to the original group object space in Figure 4 will produce the rank order of distances for sources 2′ and 4′ in Figure 5).

that the mean coordinate, "centroid," or center of gravity of each dimension of the object space is zero.) Thus, the object coordinates are constrained by this normalization, and the weights, w_{kr}, are adjusted so that the reconstructed distances on the left side of equation [2] remain unchanged. The fact that the source weights are rescaled to accommodate a rescaling of the object coordinates explains why the source weights w_{kr} *cannot* be readily interpreted as percentages relative to some baseline or as probabilities. While we have witnessed attempts by users of the INDSCAL model to attach such interpretations to the dimension weights, those efforts are completely unfounded.

However, this normalization just described for the object coordinates does confer a benefit on the resulting source (weights) space. Specifically, the square of the Euclidean distance of a source's point (in the weight space) from its origin (which coincides with the location of source 9 in the upper right panel of Figure 4) can be interpreted (approximately) as the total variance accounted for (VAF) in the respective source's data (after they have been transformed to scalar products form, as explained in Appendix B). The qualification of "approximately" is necessary in the preceding sentence because the exact variance accounted for will also depend on the correlations among object dimensions (viz., among their numerical coordinates x_{ir}). If all dimensions are orthogonal, so that all such (pairwise) product-moment correlations are zero, the square of the Euclidean distance between the source's point and the origin of the weights space will provide a direct measure of the variance accounted for by the respective source. In the source space resulting from an analysis using SINDSCAL (Pruzansky, 1975), the point representing a source will be of unit distance from the origin only if all the variance is accounted for (i.e., there is a perfect fit for that source) and the dimensions of the object space turn out empirically to be orthogonal. If the dimensions are instead correlated, the relevant distance may be less than one even though all the respective source's variance has been accounted for.

NOTEWORTHY PATTERNS OF SOURCE WEIGHTS

Considering this interpretation of a source's position vis-à-vis the origin of the source (weights) space, note in Figure 4 that although sources 3 and 7 have the same pattern of dimension weights, a higher proportion of variance is accounted for in the case of source 3 when the INDSCAL model is fitted. Since the data (after transformation to scalar product form) for sources closer to the origin generally have lesser goodness-of-fit in an application of the INDSCAL model, the dimensions of the group object space are overall less salient for these sources. The lower "communality" (see J. O. Kim and Mueller, 1978) for sources closer to the origin may result from idiosyncratic dimensions not uncovered in the R-dimensional solution, or from more random error in those sources' data.

The point for source 9 in the upper right panel of Figure 4 coincides with the origin and thus indicates that goodness-of-fit for this source was zero. Aside from the case of a source with negative weights departing markedly from zero, the situation for source 9 is the strongest evidence available to a data analyst that model misspecification has occurred. Various possible hypotheses would include totally random data or utilizing a set of dimensions completely different from those used by the other sources.

The facility of the INDSCAL model for allowing zero weights thus provides for the special case where two or more distinct groups of sources have completely different perceptual, judgmental, or other substantively-based spaces, with no dimensions in common between the two groups and thus no communality (Carroll and Wish, 1974a). This situation can be accommodated in an analysis based on the INDSCAL model by defining a group object space whose dimensions are the union of the two different groups of sources, with each subgroup of sources having nonzero weights in only one subset of dimensions. For example, if one group of sources judges the objects using Dimensions I and II while the second group of sources uses III and IV, an analysis using the INDSCAL model may accommodate these two completely discrepant "points of view" (terminology of Tucker and Messick, 1963) by using a four-dimensional solution comprising Dimensions I, II, III, and IV for the object space. Thus, Tucker and Messick's (1963) points of view approach is subsumed as a special case of the INDSCAL model. However, INDSCAL analyses are more interesting and appropriate when communality exists among the sources, as is generally the case.

A final point concerning the pattern of source weights in the results from an analysis fitting the INDSCAL model is best illustrated by returning again to the points for sources 3 and 7 in the upper right panel of Figure 4. Since these two sources had weights that were in identical proportions across the two dimensions depicted in the figure, it follows that for the part of the sources' respective matrices accounted for by these two dimensions, there was also a constant proportion between the corresponding parts. More generally, whenever we have a set of sources whose fitted weights result in points on a ray passing through the origin of the source space, there is an indeterminacy in the orientation of the corresponding plane formed by those dimensions, if most of the sources are lined up on or near that ray. (Sources 3, 7, and 9 in the upper right panel of Figure 4 form such a ray.) Recall in the Rosenberg and Kim (1975) analysis that even though we did not present a plot of the source (weights) space, the "ray" pattern was numerically evident in Table 1. Also, as we noted at that point, the SINDSCAL program also helps identify the occurrence of this problem by listing a "normalized sum of products (subjects)", as illustrated and discussed below.

A SECOND EXAMPLE: THE MILLER AND NICELY (1955) DATA

Before considering further technical details of using and fitting the INDSCAL model for data analysis, we first consider a second published example, and in more detail than given for Rosenberg and Kim (1975).

The data from a classic study by G. A. Miller and Nicely (1955) have been the subject of analyses using the Carroll-Chang INDSCAL model (Carroll and Wish, 1974a; Wish and Carroll, 1974; Soli and Arabie, 1979; Arabie and Soli, 1982) as well as other three-way spatial models (Kroonenberg and de Leeuw, 1980; DeSarbo and Carroll, 1985) and clustering (Soli, Arabie, and Carroll, 1986). (Still other analyses may be found in Hubert, 1972, Shepard, 1972b, 1974, 1980, Carroll and Wish, 1974b, and Shepard and Arabie, 1979.) A general review of the many analyses this classic data set has supported is given by Shepard (1987). The presentation here is a summary of the analyses given in Soli and Arabie (1979) and Arabie and Soli (1982). The data from Miller and Nicely's (1955) experiment consist of 17 full 16×16 matrices of identification confusions between 16 consonant phonemes, which are the "objects" in this analysis. These analyses all assume that the more confusable a pair of stimuli are found to be, the more similar they are. The identification responses of five female subjects were obtained in $K = 17$ different listening conditions, which are the "sources" of the proximity matrices. Four of the subjects listened while a fifth subject served as a speaker, reading lists of consonant vowel syllables formed by pairing the consonants /b, d, g, p, t, k, m, n, v, ð, z, ʒ, f, θ, s, ∫ / with the vowel /a/. (The phonemes $\theta, \eth, \int$, and ʒ are respectively pronounced as in *th*in, *th*at, *sh*awl, *Zh*ivago.) The subjects rotated as speaker and listeners within each experimental condition. The listeners recorded the consonant they heard after each syllable was spoken.

The 17 sources of experimental conditions are summarized in Table 2 and may be classified under three headings. First were the noise-masking conditions in which only the signal-to-noise (S/N) ratio changed. The S/N ratio was manipulated by varying the amplitude of random noise which had been low-pass filtered at 6500 Hz. Second were the low-pass conditions in which a constant S/N ratio of 12 dB was maintained while the speech was low-pass filtered at the cutoff frequencies given in Table 2. Finally, were high-pass conditions in which the same constant S/N ratio of 12 dB was again maintained while the speech channel was high-pass filtered at the cutoff frequencies also given in Table 2.

Each of the 17 matrices of confusions (listed by Miller and Nicely, 1955, pp. 340-345) contains many departures from symmetry (that is, there are many instances where $\delta_{ij,k} \neq \delta_{ji,k}$), so that the raw data are not immediately suitable for fitting by the INDSCAL model. Explicit details on how the data were symmetrized and transformed are given in the Appendix of Arabie and Soli (1982) and will not be reproduced here. Also, we should note that the published analyses (Soli and

TABLE 2

Experimental Conditions (Sources) and Results of Fitting
INDSCAL to the Miller-Nicely Data

Listening conditions		Weights for Dimensions				R^2
Signal-to-noise ratio (dB)	Bandwidth (Hz)	1	2	3	4	(Proportion of variance accounted for)
Noise masking conditions						
N1, L1 12	200-6500	0.35	0.41	0.43	0.26	0.58
N2 6	200-6500	0.45	0.53	0.39	0.24	0.75
N3 0	200-6500	0.52	0.55	0.37	0.20	0.81
N4 −6	200-6500	0.62	0.52	0.20	0.17	0.78
N5 −12	200-6500	0.74	0.41	0.20	0.19	0.84
N6 −18	200-6500	0.49	0.40	0.15	0.10	0.47
Low-pass filtering conditions						
L2, H1 12	200-5000	0.39	0.54	0.41	0.26	0.73
L3 12	200-2500	0.45	0.52	0.43	0.25	0.77
L4 12	200-1200	0.54	0.52	0.33	0.10	0.73
L5 12	200-600	0.53	0.59	0.28	0.13	0.78
L6 12	200-400	0.69	0.41	0.23	0.16	0.78
L7 12	200-300	0.67	0.50	0.08	0.05	0.76
High-pass filtering conditions						
H2 12	1000-5000	0.33	0.37	0.46	0.38	0.63
H3 12	2000-5000	0.38	0.15	0.29	0.55	0.58
H4 12	2500-5000	0.25	0.21	0.29	0.56	0.53
H5 12	3000-5000	0.19	0.10	0.25	0.69	0.61
H6 12	4500-5000	0.06	0.08	0.13	0.77	0.63
Proportion of variance accounted for by each dimension		0.33	0.13	0.16	0.07	0.69

Arabie, 1979; Arabie and Soli, 1982) upon which this discussion is based were conducted in 1976, using the INDSCAL (Chang and Carroll, 1969) program. When the Miller-Nicely data were analyzed with SINDSCAL on a computer different from that used in 1976, we found very slight differences in the solution (e.g., 69.07% variance accounted for in the reanalysis versus 69.22% in the original). To maintain consistency with the earlier published accounts, we are presenting the INDSCAL program's output in the format used by SINDSCAL.

Interpretation of Miller-Nicely Object Space. Scaling solutions from six dimensions through one dimension produced the variances accounted for below in Table 3. While there are no general or absolute criteria for determining the appropriate dimensionality when fitting the INDSCAL model, a variety of substantively technical considerations as well as comparisons with earlier analyses led Soli and Arabie to select their four-dimensional solution. Presenting all six two-dimensional projections of this object space and the same number for the source space would require too much space in virtually any published account; hence, Soli and Arabie (1979; Arabie and Soli, 1982) presented only selected projections. Figures 6a and 6b reproduce Dimensions 1 versus 2 and 3 versus 4. Please note that the broken horizontal and vertical lines in these figures were interpretively positioned to segregate the consonant phonemes.

Soli and Arabie (1979; Arabie and Soli, 1982) provided an elaborate interpretation of the spatial solution for the 16 consonant phonemes used by Miller and Nicely (1955), and only a summary is reported here. Readers wishing more detail should consult those references. On the other hand, readers whose substantive interests are remote from the area of speech perception may wish to skip ahead to the interpretation of the source space, since that section assumes much less substantive background and contains a methodologically novel approach to this interpretive task. [Although limitations of space preclude giving a detailed bibliography of such applications in other substantive areas, some noteworthy sources include (a) Nygren and L. E. Jones (1977) and Coxon (1982, pp. 190-202) in political science, (b) Schiffman, Reynolds, and Young (1981) in psychophysics, (c) Wish (1976; Wish and Kaplan, 1977) in social psychology, (d) reviews by Shepard (1987) and Shoben and Ross (in press) in cognitive psychology, and (e) Coxon and C. L. Jones (1977, 1978, 1979a, 1979b) in sociology.] It is our impression that most data analysts fitting the INDSCAL model spend considerable time interpreting the object space (usually with success) but much less time on the source space. Since we believe the latter is also deserving of attention, we will elaborate more on it.

The first dimension of the object space appears to specify the temporal relationship between onset of periodic formant resonance and the initiation of broadly dispersed acoustic energy. An attempt to capture this generality led Soli and Arabie to select the abbreviated label "periodicity/burst order."

In choosing a label for the second dimension, the perceptual weights for this dimension in all listening conditions were also examined (see Table 2). The pattern of weights implied that the second dimension specified spectral changes in the lower portion of the speech spectrum that are excited by relatively large amounts of acoustic energy, corresponding to "first formant transitions," which becomes the label for the second dimension.

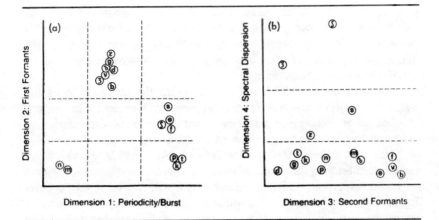

Figure 6: Two projections from the four-dimensional "group" object space resulting from fitting the INDSCAL model to the Miller-Nicely data. The broken lines partition the planes into regions corresponding to distinguishable acoustic characteristics of the syllables. (Reproduced with permission from Soli and Arabie, 1979, p. 51.)

The third dimension of Figure 6b seems to specify the shape of voiced second formant transitions in the syllables, and resembles the dimension in Wish's analysis (Carroll and Wish, 1974a; Wish and Carroll, 1974) labeled "second formant transitions." That label has been retained in the current analysis. The arrangement of phonemes on the fourth dimension corresponds quite well to the amount of spectrally dispersed acoustic energy located below 5 kHz in the speech spectrum. Because of this correspondence, the dimension has been given the label "spectral dispersion."

Perhaps the most succinct summary of this object space is to note that acoustic properties rather than phonetic features gave the most interpretable account of the dimensions. This conclusion differs from previous analyses and runs counter to traditional theorizing by some phoneticians. Our conclusions are reinforced by the source (weights) space, to which we now turn.

Interpretation of Miller-Nicely Source Space. An examination of the dimension weights, which gauge the perceptual effect of each dimension under the different listening conditions, can also aid in this acoustic interpretation. These weights, summarized in Table 2, may be represented in the four-dimensional source space where each point presents an experimental condition with the fitted dimension weights as coordinates. The configuration of points in the condition space is depicted in Figure 7. Noise-masking conditions are represented in the figures by the labels N1-N6, and the high- and low-pass conditions by H1-H6 and L1-L7, respectively.

The numbers in these labels increase with the degradation of the signal by progressively greater masking noise or filtering. The pattern of changes in perceptual importance with increasing degradation is indicated by the arrows superimposed on the configurations of points.

Soli and Arabie (1979; Arabie and Soli, 1982) provided an elaborate substantive interpretation of the source (weight) space, based on visual inspection, and that interpretation will not be repeated here. Instead, we will focus on those authors' efforts to relate the weights to the exogenous information given by the defining characteristics of the experimental conditions (i.e., sources), namely the physical parameters specifying the kind and degree of acoustic degradation imposed on the speech signal in each condition (source). Thus, the dimension weights may also be presented directly as a function of these parameters (viz., S/N ratio, low-pass cutoff frequency, and high-pass cutoff frequency) for high- and low-pass conditions.

Weights for the first formant dimension are presented graphically in Figure 8(a) and for the second formant dimension in Figure 8(b) for both high- and low-pass conditions. In the experimental design the crucial difference between the different low-pass conditions was that low-pass cutoffs were varied while the high-pass cutoff was held constant at 200 Hz. The reverse was true for high-pass conditions, where high-pass cutoffs were varied while the low-pass cutoffs were held constant at 5 kHz. (See Table 2.) The variable cutoff frequencies for both low- and high-pass conditions are given on the horizontal axes of Figures 8(a) and 8(b). As an aid to interpretation, the smooth functions were fitted manually to the weights in the plot. By examining changes in weights as a function of changing cutoffs, the boundaries of the spectral region containing cues for each dimension may be ascertained. The regions respectively comprise 200 to 800 Hz for the first formant and 1 to 3 kHz for the second formant.

The first and fourth dimensions [periodicity/burst order and spectral dispersion, respectively, in Figures 9(a) and 9(b)] exhibit very different patterns of weights from those reported for the formant transitions in Figure 8. The high- and low-pass functions do not intersect. Instead, the importance of periodicity/burst information (Dimension 1) in low-pass conditions is least with minimal degradation, and increases consistently as the bandwidth narrows, suggesting that this acoustic property acquires its perceptual importance only as formant information

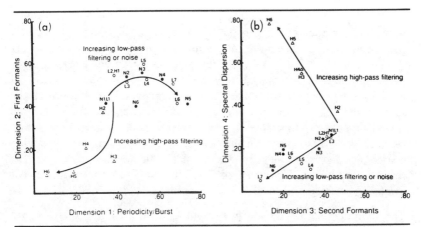

Figure 7: Projections of the sources' coordinates for Dimensions 1 and 2 (left panel) and 3 and 4 (right panel). Noise-masking, low-pass filtering, and high-pass filtering conditions are denoted by filled circles, open circles, and open triangles, respectively. Condition numbers increase with increasing degradation of the signal within each set of conditions. The arrows show the pattern of changing dimension weights within sets of listening conditions. As pointed out by Mark Kinnucan, earlier published versions of the figure in the left panel erroneously reversed the labels "L6" and "L7". (Adapted from Soli and Arabie, 1979, p. 54.)

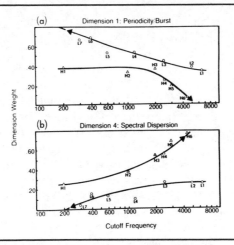

Figure 8: Weights for sources (experimental conditions) plotted as a function of cutoff frequency for Dimensions 1 (upper panel) and 4 (lower panel). The smooth functions were fitted manually. For the high-pass conditions, denoted by triangles, degradation increases with increasing high-pass cutoff frequencies in the direction of the arrow superimposed on the function, i.e., from left to right in the figure. For low-pass conditions, denoted by circles, degradation increases with decreasing low-pass cutoff frequencies in the opposite direction, from right to left in the figure. (Reproduced with permission from Soli and Arabie, 1979, p. 55.)

in Dimensions 2 and 3 becomes unavailable because of signal degradation. Spectral dispersion (Dimension 4) in Figure 9(b) has a pattern of weights resembling that found for the periodicity/burst order (Dimension 1). Dimension 4 has its greatest perceptual effect in high-pass conditions under the most severe degradation, while in relatively good listening conditions, it has the least perceptual importance of the four dimensions. The pattern of condition weights for both the periodicity/burst (Dimension 1) and spectral dispersion (Dimension 4) reveals that these acoustic properties are important in specifying consonant phoneme identity when such other perceptual cues as formant transitions (emphasized in Dimensions 2 and 3) are not available.

The Role of Source Weights in Presenting an INDSCAL Analysis. As should be clear by now, it is the weights, **W**, in the INDSCAL model that distinguish this model of three-way MDS from two-way MDS and that confer the unique orientation of the axes in the object space **X**. One way of viewing the $K \times R$ fitted parameters constituting **W** is that they simply provide the unique orientation of **X**. We generally reject this view and argue instead that the data analyst has a responsibility to attempt to offer a convincing interpretation of these fitted parameters. If they are not interpretable, then the use of two-way MDS may be more appropriate for the particular data set.

The analysis in the sections immediately preceding this one provided a detailed interpretation of the source weights. Another elaborate interpretation of such weights is given in studies by Bisanz, LaPorte, Vesonder, and Voss (1978), LaPorte and Voss (1979), and Bisanz and Voss (1982).

Now that we have completed the description of Soli and Arabie's (1979) analysis of the Miller-Nicely (1955) data, using the INDSCAL model, it is appropriate to consider one aspect of what the SINDSCAL program (Pruzansky, 1975) is doing while fitting the model to these data. Appendix B of this monograph gives a detailed technical description of the algorithm embodied in that program.

The INDSCAL model (Equation [2]) is not easily fitted directly to the three-way input proximity matrix **Δ**. Carroll and Chang (1970) observed that the model could be fitted much more readily to *scalar products* (described in Appendix B) based on **Δ**; thus, those authors' (Chang and Carroll, 1969) INDSCAL program, for fitting the model of the same name, began with transforming the proximity values in **Δ** to scalar products. Pruzansky's (1975) SINDSCAL also follows this same approach. (Such other programs as ALSCAL by Takane, Young, and de Leeuw, 1977, and described here in Appendix D, and

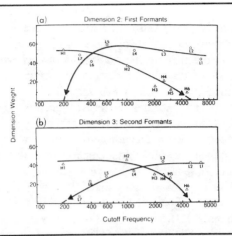

Figure 9: Weights for sources (experimental conditions) plotted as a function of cutoff frequency for Dimensions 2 (upper panel) and 3 (lower panel). The smooth functions were fitted manually. For the high-pass conditions, denoted by triangles, degradation increases with increasing high-pass cutoff frequencies in the direction of the arrow superimposed on the function, i.e., from left to right in the figure. For low-pass conditions, denoted by circles, degradation increases with decreasing low-pass cutoff frequencies in the opposite direction, from right to left in the figure. (Reproduced with permission from Soli and Arabie, 1979, p. 55.)

MULTISCALE by Ramsay, 1977, 1978a, 1978b, 1980, 1981, 1982b, 1983, and described here in Appendix C, do not use scalar products for fitting the INDSCAL model, but instead fit the model to the input similarities or dissimilarities, possibly transformed by monotonic functions.) Because SINDSCAL and the earlier INDSCAL programs both fit the model to these scalar products, all the values previously reported in this paper for goodness-of-fit concern variance accounted for (VAF) in the scalar products, rather than in the proximities data on which those scalar products are based.

4. DECISIONS TO BE MADE IN RUNNING SINDSCAL ANALYSES

MATRIX (UN)CONDITIONALITY

Carroll and Chang (1970, pp. 288-289) noted that in preliminary work on developing the INDSCAL program, a situation arose where one subject's (i.e., source's) proximity matrix contained much larger entries than did the other sources', with the result that the heavy-handed source's data dominated the analysis. To correct for such situations, those authors (Chang and Carroll, 1969) wrote the

INDSCAL program so that its default option automatically multiplied each source's matrix of derived scalar products (see Appendix B) by a normalizing constant required to set the sum of squares for each matrix equal to unity. (Note that this normalization of each source's matrix of scalar products should *not* be confused with the normalization of the coordinates matrix X for the object space.) Takane et al. (1977) questioned whether this normalization was universally appropriate in fitting the INDSCAL model and introduced the useful distinction of *matrix conditional* versus *matrix unconditional* data (as defined earlier in this paper). Since Carroll and Chang's (1969) INDSCAL program implicitly assumed sources were using different numerical scales ("conditional" on a particular matrix), and thus requiring a normalization to obtain commensurate entries in the three-way input data, the original INDSCAL program always assumed matrix conditional data, as does Pruzansky's (1975) SINDSCAL program.

The ALSCAL (Takane et al., 1977) and MULTISCALE (Ramsay, 1977, 1978a, 1978b, 1980, 1981, 1982b, 1983) programs allow matrix unconditional analyses. Empirically, however, matrix unconditional analyses have shown few if any general advantages over the matrix conditional approach, and Schiffman et al. (1981, p. 175) recommend in general that the matrix conditional option be specified when using ALSCAL.

MacCallum (1977) considered the implications for matrix conditional versus unconditional analyses for the weights, W, in fitting the INDSCAL model. He concluded that for the former type of analysis, weights are only comparable within a given source's "private" solution, as ratios of pairs of dimension weights. According to MacCallum (1977), comparing weights based on data from different sources is permissible only for a matrix unconditional analysis. In effect, MacCallum's arguments imply that one should use only the directions and *not* the lengths of the vectors (formed by the origin and the points representing different sources) in an INDSCAL (matrix conditional) solution. Although we agree that the direction is the *primary* information, the secondary information given by the length has proved useful in several analyses, including data on the perception of stress patterns in English words (Wish, 1969; Wish and Carroll, 1974, pp. 462-470). In these analyses, the weights for subjects (i.e., sources of data) whose native language was not English were consistently smaller than were the weights for native speakers of English. That is, the former groups' vectors were all shorter, and these individuals' variances accounted for were less than were those of native spakers of English. It could be argued either (a) the data for the sources less well fitted required higher dimensionality, or (b) these sources' data contained more error. In either case, it was the *length* (and not the direction) of the sources' vectors that distinguished those subjects from native speakers of English. This observation about length of vectors does not hold for such programs as MULTISCALE, discussed below, that use a different normalization procedure when fitting the INDSCAL model. Users of the INDSCAL model sometimes wish to run inferential statistical tests on the sources' weights, and Schiffman et al. (1981, Ch. 13) recommended the use of "directional statistics" for this purpose. More recent research (C. L. Jones, 1983; Hubert, Golledge, Constanza, Gale, and Haleprin, 1984) has undermined that recommendation and provided more straightforward approaches for such tests. These recent results (and others given by Carroll, 1986) contradict MacCallum's (1977, p. 305) earlier abjuration of "... correlating weights with each other, correlating weights with outside [exogenous] variables, or even calculating and comparing, via t-tests or analysis of variance, mean weights for subgroups of individuals [i.e., sources]."

DIMENSIONALITY AND REQUIRED AMOUNTS OF DATA

The SINDSCAL program allows a maximum dimensionality (MAXDIM) of 10 and a minimum dimensionality (MINDIM) of 1. Concerning the former limit, it is not difficult to modify the FORTRAN source code so as to allow even higher dimensionality, although it is difficult to envisage the need for such a modification. Concerning the lower limit, obtaining a one-dimensional solution (by setting MINDIM = 1 in SINDSCAL) is a common practice, but has little more to offer than the report of variance accounted for in that least dimensionality. If all the sources are really giving the same underlying single dimension, then the only allowable difference among individual sources is a scale factor, which should have already been largely removed in the normalization of scalar products matrices. Thus, truly unidimensional data constitute a fairly uninteresting special case for the INDSCAL model, regardless of which program is used to fit it, in contrast to the situation for two-way MDS (see Carroll and Arabie, 1980, p. 617).

Concerning selection of the appropriate number of dimensions in three-way MDS, from a set of solutions ranging from MAXDIM down to MINDIM dimensions, there are no universally accepted criteria, only various strategies. It is traditional to plot increments in VAF for SINDSCAL (and decrements in SSTRESS for ALSCAL, discussed below) as solutions are considered in successively higher dimensions, just as in factor analysis or in two-way MDS for "stress," and then to look for an "elbow" in the plot, indicating that additional dimensions made negligible improvements in goodness-of-fit. (The information is given in Table 3, for the Soli-Arabie analysis of the Miller-Nicely data.) In practice, the elbow is as ubiquitous as the Holy Grail, and this strategy rarely provides a decisive answer. Moreover, when inspecting such a plot, one is implicitly assuming that linear scaling is appropriate both for dimensionality and VAF. (Ramsay's quite different and innovative approach in MULTISCALE to this problem is discussed below.)

Yet another aspect of spatial dimensionality in fitting the INDSCAL model concerns orthogonality of axes in the object space. Although the axes provided by running SINDSCAL generally turn out to be orthogonal or nearly so, there is no requirement in either the INDSCAL model or the SINDSCAL program that the axes be so constrained. Perhaps it should be added that unlike the situation with rotations in factor analysis, the user has no control over the empirical question of whether INDSCAL dimensions turn out to be orthogonal. Under the heading "SUM OF PRODUCTS (STIMULI)," SINDSCAL lists a lower triangular halfmatrix of cosines between all pairs of axes for the objects ("stimuli"). (Perhaps a better heading for this matrix would be "sum of cross-products" since each entry, for dimensions r and r', is just the sum of pairwise products of object coordinates $[x_{ir} x_{ir'}]$ computed over objects, $i = 1 \cdots I$.) The matrix resulting from the Soli-Arabie analysis of the Miller-Nicely data is given immediately below. Note that all diagonal entries are 1.0, since the angle between an axis and itself is zero, corresponding to a cosine of 1.0. (Orthogonal dimensions, of course, would have a cosine of 0.)

SUM OF PRODUCTS (STIMULI)

1	1.000			
2	.266	1.000		
3	.034	.008	1.000	
4	.089	−.055	−.242	1.000

In general, dimensionality is often decided on the basis of substantive interpretability of dimensions. Such interpretation should be focused on *both* the object space *and* the source space. For verbally labeling dimensions in the object space, the strategies Kruskal and Wish (1978, pp. 35-36, 57, and Appendix A) and Coxon (1982, Ch. 4) discuss of using multiple linear regression (e.g., via Chang and Carroll's, 1968, PROFIT program, or Meulman, Heiser, and Carroll's, 1987, PREFMAP3 with various options for plotting and regression) are also useful. Additional strategies are applied by Nygren and

L. E. Jones (1977). Because, in contrast to two-way MDS, the approach taken in fitting the INDSCAL model uses K input proximity matrices and produces two separate (but interrelated) spatial solutions, one for the objects and one for the sources, it is exceedingly difficult to devise valid general-purpose guidelines for dimensionality (R) as a function of I, K, and VAF, but first steps have been taken (Weinberg & Carroll, 1986). Monte Carlo studies (i.e., numerical experiments using simulated data) have also been made, using highly specific assumptions about the type of data collected (e.g., L. E. Jones and Dong, 1980) and error models assumed.

Stating the number of objects (I) required to justify selection of an R-dimensional solution is much more problematic than for two-way MDS (Kruskal and Wish, 1978, p. 52), where there is only $K = 1$ input proximity matrix. Empirically, published applications using the INDSCAL model have tended toward higher dimensionalities than is the case for two-way MDS, where the upper limit is typically three. (See Shepard's [1974, pp. 385-391] emphasis on being able to visualize two-way solutions.) For example, Chang and Carroll (1980) published a seven-dimensional solution for the perception of color. Some methodological support for such high-dimensional solutions comes from studies with many more than just $K = 1$ input matrices (as used in two-way MDS), so that more data are supporting a higher-dimensional solution.

Stating the number of sources (K) required to confer a unique orientation of the axes in the object space is another unresolved issue. In principle, as few as $K = 2$ may suffice (the SINDSCAL program should not be run with $K < 2$), but even an infinite number would be inadequate if all the input proximity matrices differed only by a scalar multiple (i.e., were all related to each other by similarity transformations).

NUMBER OF ITERATIONS

It is important to remember that during the iterative progress of the alternating least squares procedure in SINDSCAL, both the object coordinates X and the source coordinates (weights) are being solved for. During the early development of both the INDSCAL (Chang and Carroll, 1969) and SINDSCAL (Pruzansky, 1975) programs, it was noticed that the object space (X) was generally much more robust than was the source space (W). That is, as adjustments and refinements were made in the algorithms, the object space for a given set of data seemed much less affected by such changes than did the source space. Intuitively, we believe that the first few iterations of SINDSCAL readily solve for X, but that relatively much more effort is required to

TABLE 3

Variance Accounted for as a Function of
Dimensionality for INDSCAL Solutions on
Log-transformed Miller-Nicely Data

Dimensionality	VAF	Increment
1	0.33	
		0.13
2	0.46	
		0.16
3	0.62	
		0.07
4	0.69	
		0.04
5	0.73	
		0.04
6	0.77	

obtain the object space's unique orientation that is conferred by the source space (**W**). For this reason, we suspect that users whose SINDSCAL analyses run for only a few iterations may be misled into assuming that because the object configuration (divorced from its orientation) is acceptably interpretable, that only extra computational expense and no substantive benefits would accrue from further iterations. Indeed, the original INDSCAL (Chang and Carroll, 1969) program's documentation recommended setting an upper limit of only 15 or 20 iterations.

Recall that although the user stipulates the maximum number of iterations (parameter ITMAX, on the second control "card"), the number of iterations the program uses may be terminated earlier if the program determines that only a negligible improvement (.000001 in the August, 1982, version of SINDSCAL) in an error term results from a given iteration. When the program prints a message stating that the maximum number of iterations (specified by the user) has been reached, it is important to check whether VAF was still increasing appreciably during the last iterations. If the increases were well above the program's built-in criterion for convergence, the user may wish to rerun the analysis with a larger value of ITMAX. (If the user declared a value of either 2 or 3 for IPUNCH on the second parameter card, the run can be resumed with the numerical values computed on the last completed iteration that was a multiple of 10.) Note also that just beneath the section labeled "HISTORY OF COMPUTATION" is a two-line section, with the second line beginning "FINAL [iteration]," as shown in Table 4. The penultimate column for that line gives the final VAF by the overall solution. That VAF should be equal or nearly so to the VAF printed just above it for the penultimate iteration. (For the

SINDSCAL run of Miller-Nicely data, the respective entries for VAF are .692250 and .692251.) If the final value of VAF differs by more than about 2%, then at the time the SINDSCAL program equated the two estimates of the object coordinates X (see discussion of B and C in equations B.22 through B.26 in Appendix B), there were sufficient discrepancies between the two estimates that goodness-of-fit suffered by equating them. Since the two are asymptotically identical, the drop in VAF is evidence of premature termination of the iterative procedure.

INITIAL (OR "STARTING") CONFIGURATION

The initial configuration refers to the starting values used for X, the matrix with I rows and R columns (shown in the left panel of Figure 3) whose entries are coordinates of the objects. (There is no counterpart starting configuration for the source or weights space.) When the user specifies IRN $= 0$, Pruzansky's (1975) SINDSCAL actually reads and prints the *transpose* (X') of X. Unless the user has specified ITMAX $= 0$ and (necessarily) supplied the X' matrix, so that W (only) is being solved for in a single pass, a good rule is as follows: Always begin with MAXDIM (the maximum dimensionality) at least two dimensions more than would be expected, on substantive grounds, to be adopted for the final solution. (Recall that 10 is the upper limit set for MAXDIM in SINDSCAL.) This practice can help in diagnosing and thus eliminating problems of local minima that sometimes hinder the optimization procedures in SINDSCAL.

Specifying IRN as a positive four-digit integer results in a random initial configuration for X (and those values are printed as X' in SINDSCAL's output, in a format identical to that when X' is user-supplied). Using several different random initial configurations, by specifying different positive values of IRN on different runs, is a strategy that has worked well for nonmetric two-way MDS (Arabie, 1973, 1978a, 1978b), and Carroll (1985) has advocated its use in fitting the INDSCAL model. In particular, he recommended this strategy in preference to deriving a rational initial configuration from the output of a two-way scaling program that used data aggregated over the K sources (and supplying the coordinates to SINDSCAL via the IRN $= 0$ option). Although 1970-1980 saw considerable research on providing rational initial configurations for INDSCAL analyses (summarized and evaluated by Carroll and Arabie, 1980, p. 632), very little exportable software for this purpose has been written.

When several different random initial configurations are used, the user should tabulate VAF for each dimensionality (from MAXDIM to MINDIM) for each run of the program. (Note that only the MAXDIM-dimensional solutions start directly with the randomly generated values in **X**. For each subsequent solution of progressively lower dimensionality, SINDSCAL uses the previous solution after dropping the dimension accounting for the least variance.) If several runs all have the same VAF for a given dimensionality, the solutions are probably identical as well, although the spaces may differ by a reflection and/or permutation of the axes. If the VAF for two solutions for the same data in the same dimensionality is equal to three or four decimal places, the solutions are probably identical, even though strictly speaking, such agreement is a necessary but not sufficient condition for identical solutions in the given dimensionality.

CONSTRAINED SOLUTIONS

Specifying that ITMAX $= 0$ and giving a user-supplied initial configuration (by setting IRN $= 0$ and supplying the **X**′ matrix immediately after the K-th proximity matrix in the input for SINDSCAL) allows the user to *constrain* the object space (**X**) to have numerical coordinates specified by the user, so that a one-pass fitting of the source weights (**W**) is executed via the multiple linear regression routine in SINDSCAL. This option is applicable when the user has an a priori-derived object configuration (**X**) and only lacks the weights (**W**) and goodness-of-fit (VAF). Note, however, that the resulting weights are more vulnerable to negative (and thus uninterpretable) values than when both **W** and **X** have been fitted iteratively in an unconstrained analysis.

The zero iterations option (ITMAX $= 0$) in SINDSCAL offers merely one of the simplest forms of constrained INDSCAL representations. Research on more complex forms (e.g., by Bloxom, 1978) is summarized by Carroll and Arabie (1980, pp. 633-634). Ramsay's (1977, 1978a, 1978b, 1980, 1981, 1982b, 1983) MULTISCALE II provides the greatest facility for producing more general constrained solutions.

VARIANCE ACCOUNTED FOR (VAF)

VAF in the SINDSCAL program's approach to fitting the INDSCAL model is computed as

$$VAF = 1 - \frac{\sum_{k=1}^{K} \sum_i \sum_j (b_{ij,k} - \hat{b}_{ij,k})^2}{\sum_{k=1}^{K} \sum_i \sum_j (b_{ij,k} - b_{..,k})^2} \qquad [4]$$

where $b_{ij,k}$ is the scalar product derived from Δ_k for objects i and j, using the k-th source's proximity matrix, and $\hat{b}_{ij,k}$ is the corresponding

TABLE 4

Excerpt of INDSCAL Miller-Nicely Analysis

HISTORY OF COMPUTATION

ITERATION	CORRELATIONS BETWEEN Y(DATA) AND YHAT	VAF (R**2)	LOSS (Y-YHAT)**2
0	.770741	.594041	.405959
1	.791846	.627020	.372980
2	.817867	.668907	.331093
3	.827246	.684336	.315664
4	.829960	.688834	.311166
5	.831017	.690590	.309410
6	.831510	.691408	.308592
7	.831758	.691821	.308179
8	.831888	.692037	.307963
9	.931957	.692153	.307847
10	.831995	.692216	.307784
11	.832016	.692250	.307750
REACHED CRITERION ON ITERATION 11			
FINAL	.832016	.692251	.307749

estimated scalar product derived from the fitted model. (See Appendix B and the earlier discussion on matrix conditionality for details.) The term $b_{..k}$ simply refers to the arithmetic mean of all the scalar products for distinct pairs of objects for the k-th source's data.

Equation [4] is used to compute VAF over all K sources of data, but it can be applied separately as well to the scalar products matrix for each (single) source of data by restricting the outer summation in the numerator and denominator to apply *only* to data from each (single) source. The SINDSCAL program prints the square root of VAF for each source under the heading "CORRELATION BETWEEN COMPUTED SCORES AND SCALAR PROD. FOR SUBJECTS." These values are squared and reported as VAF by source (experimental condition) in the rightmost column of Table 2.

If any of the sources are outliers vis-à-vis VAF by sources, the data analyst may wish to give additional scrutiny to the data from such source(s). In particular, if the VAF is especially worse than for other sources (possibly coinciding with negative source weights), the data analyst may wish to consider rerunning the analysis after excluding data from the offending source(s).

It should be noted that if two or more sources have identical or very similar variances accounted for in fitting the INDSCAL model, this fact does *not* imply that the corresponding solutions are identical: very different patterns of weights for the sources' (common) dimensions could still produce identical values of VAF for such sources.

Not only can VAF be looked at by source but also by increment per additional dimension as one looks at the solutions in the reverse order of their generation. The SINDSCAL output (not reproduced here) and the last line of Table 2 report these increments. In the former location, for example, under the heading "APPROXIMATE PROPORTION OF TOTAL VARIANCE ACCOUNTED FOR BY EACH DIMENSION," one can note that adding the fourth dimension increased VAF by 7%, from 62 to 69%. The heading includes the qualification "APPROXIMATE" because, if the dimensions of the object space are not perfectly orthogonal (see description above of "SUM OF PRODUCTS (STIMULI)" under the section on dimensionality), then the additive decomposition of VAF by dimension is only approximate. As this particular consideration of VAF attests, it and dimensionality are inseparably linked in many ways. For that reason, additional comments on VAF can be found in the earlier section on Dimensionality.

ADDITIONAL POINTS CONCERNING SINDSCAL'S OUTPUT

Under the heading "NORMALIZED SOLUTION," SINDSCAL prints the W' and X' matrices, which give the coordinates in the $r(r-1)/2$ pages of plots of the objects' and (separately) of the sources' spaces. The reader may easily verify the correspondence between the dimensions by sources (W' under the heading "SUBJECTS WEIGHTS MATRIX") and dimensions by objects (X' under the heading "STIMULUS MATRIX") with, respectively, the plots for the weight space and the object space.

Another important matrix is the lower triangular halfmatrix printed under "NORMALIZED SUM OF PRODUCTS (SUBJECTS)," (where "subjects" correspond to sources) with diagonal entries of unity as shown immediately below from the analysis of the Miller-Nicely data. It is very important not to confuse this halfmatrix with the superficially similar "SUM OF PRODUCTS (STIMULI)" discussed earlier. (Perhaps a better heading for this matrix would be "sum of cross-products" since each entry, for dimensions r and r', is just the sum of pairwise products of source coordinates $[w_{kr} \, w_{kr'}]$ computed over sources, $k = 1 \cdots K$.) If any off-diagonal entries are also close to unity, then the corresponding pair of dimensions in the object space form a plane whose orientation vis-à-vis the other dimension is *not* unique. (Recall that this situation actually arose for Dimensions 1 and 2 of Rosenberg and Kim's, 1975, object space that was presented earlier in Figure 2. In a reanalysis we conducted of the Rosenberg and Kim data, the value corresponding to Dimensions 1 and 2 was .993.) All off-diagonal entries in this matrix should lie on the interval between zero and one. The former value (hardly ever observed for real data) indicates that a unique orientation for the particular plane has definitely been achieved. There are no definitive guidelines for just how close to unity an entry must be before the data analyst decides that a plane with nonunique orientation has arisen. Scrutinizing the printer plot for the corresponding pair of dimensions in the source space, to discern a ray passing through the origin is yet another strategy for (subjectively) assessing the extent of this problem when it arises. This strategy applies to output from programs that normalize sources' weights according to the procedure described above for the INDSCAL and SINDSCAL programs.

NORMALIZED SUM OF PRODUCTS (SUBJECTS)

1	1.000			
2	.959	1.000		
3	.841	.903	1.000	
4	.576	.561	.758	1.000

DIAGNOSTICS

Perhaps the most obvious sign of trouble in running SINDSCAL is when a large proportion of the sources' weights are negative (and not close to zero). This situation usually indicates that the user has erroneously declared similarities to be dissimilarities (or vice versa) when defining IRDATA. If no such mistake has been made, then the user may question how compatible the data are with the INDSCAL model. Another problem is signaled when VAF does not increase monotonically with dimensionality. When this relationship is non-monotone, a local (rather than global) optimum has been achieved in at least one dimensionality in the range from maximum to minimum dimensionality, and the remedy is to use one or preferably several different (alternative) initial configurations for X, and possibly to increase the maximum dimensionality (but not beyond 10 in SINDSCAL) as well. Other such potential diagnostics as premature termination of the iterative procedure (when the user has allowed too few iterations) and nonunique orientation of planes (indicated by off-diagonal entries near unity in the normalized sum of products matrix for subjects) have already been discussed.

Strictly speaking, the INDSCAL model, as discussed in the preceding pages, is not falsifiable, if the dimensionality is allowed to be high and a sufficiently large constant is added to the dissimilarity data values (see de Leeuw and Heiser, 1982). There are no inferential statistical tests available for determining (overall) model misspecification or, for programs other than MULTISCALE, even whether the dimensionality of the solution adopted is correct. While some readers may find this situation disturbing, it is common to a wide range of multivariate techniques for exploratory data analysis, including many approaches to clustering and factor analysis. (However, in the case of two-way nonmetric MDS, Brady [1985] has recently made very impressive progress on the general problem.) In the next section of this paper, we will discuss other three-way MDS procedures including Ramsay's (1977, 1978a, 1978b, 1980, 1981, 1982b, 1983) MULTISCALE program, which uses a maximum likelihood approach to fitting the INDSCAL model and offers the parametric inferential tests generally associated with that estimation procedure.

5. OTHER THREE-WAY MDS SPATIAL REPRESENTATIONS

THE IDIOSCAL MODEL AND SOME SPECIAL CASES

Carroll and Chang (1970, pp. 305-310; 1972) proposed a more general model for weighted Euclidean spaces that subsumes the INDSCAL model as a special case. The IDIOSCAL (for Individual Differences In Orientation SCALing) model portrays differences among sources of data (e.g., individuals) by allowing each source a differential rotation of the dimensions of the object space common to all sources. The most general case of IDIOSCAL thus does not possess the dimensional uniqueness or preferred orientation of the object space that distinguishes the special case of the INDSCAL model.

The intuitive appeal of the IDIOSCAL model is demonstrated by the number of times it has been reinvented or by the various special cases of it that have been devised (e.g. "PARAFAC-2" by Harshman, 1972a, 1972b; "Three-Mode Scaling," by Tucker, 1972, and other procedures proposed by Bloxom, 1978, and by Ramsay, 1981, incorporating this general Euclidean metric, or some variant of it), and sometimes it has even been simultaneously reinvented *and* renamed (e.g., "the Generalized Euclidean Model" by Young, 1984). In the IDIOSCAL model, the recovered distance $d_{ij,k}$ between objects i and j for the k-th source of data is given by

$$d_{ij,k} = \sqrt{\sum_r^R \sum_{r'}^R (x_{ir} - x_{jr}) \, c_{rr'k} \, (x_{ir'} - x_{jr'})} \qquad [5]$$

where r and r' are indices of the R dimensions in the object space and (separately) the source space. This model differs mainly from the INDSCAL model of equation [2] by the inclusion of matrix

$C_k \equiv \{c_{rr'k}\}$, which is an $R \times R$ symmetric positive definite or semidefinite matrix. If C is constrained to be a diagonal matrix with nonnegative entries, then they are interpretable as source weights in the INDSCAL formulation of distance, and the INDSCAL model follows as a special case. This result can be seen by noting that if, in equation [5], $c_{rr'k} = w_{rk}$ when $r = r'$, and 0 when $r \neq r'$, then the terms $(x_{ir} - x_{jr})(x_{ir'} - x_{jr'})$ drop out if $r \neq r'$ and become $(x_{ir} - x_{jr})^2$ for $r = r'$, thus producing the INDSCAL model of equation [2]. In the (general) IDIOSCAL model, C_k provides a rotation of the object space to a new (or IDIOsyncratic) coordinate system for source k. In the Carroll and Chang (1970, pp. 305-310; 1972) approach to interpreting the model, this rotation will be orthogonal. In the alternative approach suggested independently by Tucker (1972) and by Harshman (1972a, 1972b), there is no rotation as such. Instead, the interpretation suggested by Tucker and Harshman entails differing correlations (or, more geometrically, cosines of angles) between the same dimensions of the object space, over different sources. (Further details on the two strategies are given by Carroll and Wish, 1974a, and in the source articles; also see de Leeuw and Heiser, 1982.)

In spite of the considerable intuitive appeal of the INDIOSCAL model, it has empirically yielded disappointing results in general. A major practical drawback of using the IDIOSCAL model is the potential need to provide a separate figure (or set of them) for each source's spatial representation. Nonetheless, the MULTISCALE and ALSCAL·4 packages include software (more readily exportable than the original program by Carroll and Chang, 1972) for fitting this model.

PARAFAC-1

Harshman's (1970, 1972a, Harshman and Lundy, 1984, Lundy and Harshman, 1985) PARAFAC-1 computer program (for PARAlell FACtors) for fitting the PARAFAC/CONDECOMP model can be used to fit the INDSCAL model, after appropriate pre-processing of the data. This approach to three-way factor (or components) analysis was also proposed by Carroll and Chang (1970) as the CANDECOMP for (CANonical DECOMPosition) model underlying what is called (see Appendix B) the *scalar product* form of the INDSCAL model. CANDECOMP is a general model for N-way data arrays. When limited to the three-way case, it results in a model equivalent to Harshman's PARAFAC model — often referred to for that reason as the PARAFAC/CANDECOMP (or vice-versa) model. When this general model is further restricted to a data array symmetric in two of its three ways (both corresponding to the object "mode" for data appropriate to the INDSCAL model), PARAFAC/CANDECOMP becomes equivalent to the scalar product form of INDSCAL.

Together with ancillary software provided by Lundy and Harshman (1985), the most recent version of PARAFAC may be used to fit the INDSCAL model using virtually the same steps outlined in equations [B.1] through [B.18] of Appendix B. There thus is an analogy between the salience weights for sources, the object coordinates, and corresponding parameters in PARAFAC/CANDECOMP. Correlation coefficients and possibly some types of similarity judgments can be directly modeled via such a scalar product model; Ekman (1963) discussed such scalar product models for similarities in the two-way case. Also see Harshman and Lundy (1984) for a further discussion of the relations among INDSCAL, PARAFAC, and (three-way) CANDECOMP.

MULTISCALE

Ramsay's (1977, 1978a, 1978b, 1980, 1981, 1982b, 1983) MULTISCALE is a package of programs for MDS analyses, including two-way Euclidean (as in Equation [3]), the three-way MDS in fitting the INDSCAL (equation [2]) and IDIOSCAL (equation [5]) models. MULTISCALE's reliance on maximum likelihood estimation techniques for fitting the object coordinates and source weights qualifies it more as a method of confirmatory analysis than as an exploratory technique, thus making it an exception to the other approaches discussed in this paper. In fact, Ramsay (1981, p. 390) notes that many users may wish to employ MULTISCALE as the second stage in an MDS analysis, after one of the other more exploratory programs discussed in this paper has been used. Appendix C presents a summary of the technical details of MULTISCALE in fitting the INDSCAL model.

MULTISCALE's use of maximum likelihood estimation requires the user to make strong assumptions about the nature of random variation in the input proximity data, and about the relationship of parameters of this distribution to parameters defining the underlying spatial representation. Ramsay allows the data analyst to choose from among several alternatives and distributions (e.g., lognormal, normal, and others). Because of the number of additional strong assumptions made concerning the data (e.g., that noise is independently and identically distributed in the data), MULTISCALE offers a variety of diagnostic plots for the user to inspect for graphical evidence of violated assumptions. (For an elegant summary of the statistical basis of this approach, see Ramsay, 1982a.)

MULTISCALE allows the user to select from among three classes of transformations it will perform on the data (originally assumed to be interval or ratio scale) in order to accommodate the assumptions entailed by maximum likelihood estimation to improve the fit: (a) scale factor, (b) power transformation, and (c) monotone transformation using integrated *B*-splines (Ramsay, 1981, p. 394). In addition, the user has the option of specifying an a priori transformation. The program allows the user to declare explicitly which input data values (if any) are missing. When fitting the INDSCAL model (called Model M3 in Ramsay, 1981, p. 212), MULTISCALE assumes the input data are matrix conditional, just as in Pruzansky's (1975) SINDSCAL.

MULTISCALE has one other noteworthy property vis-à-vis the subject weights. Since the likelihood function is so defined as to be invariant under multiplication of the reconstructed distances for each source by a positive constant (a fact intimately tied to the assumption of matrix conditionality), the source weight vectors are all normalized to have unit length. Thus in MULTISCALE (unlike the INDSCAL or SINDSCAL programs, even under assumptions of matrix conditionality) the interpretation of squared length of the source vector as an index of goodness-of-fit for that source does not obtain.

We noted earlier that for goodness-of-fit, SINDSCAL computes the variance accounted for (VAF) in scalar products derived from the sources' input proximity data. Although no tenable assumptions concerning an underlying distribution are known, VAF is a familiar quantity for many data analysts. In contrast, MULTISCALE uses the logarithm of the likelihood of getting the particular set of object coordinates and source weights for the given input data. Unlike VAF, the (negative) log likelihood is not bounded (above), but is useful in making inferential comparisons between pairs of different MULTISCALE solutions for the same input data set. An AIC (Akaike, 1974) and BIC (Schwartz, 1978) statistic are also calculated in MULTISCALE to adjust the log likelihood for the number of parameters. This program also allows the user much more latitude in constraining solutions than does the zero iterations option (discussed above) in SINDSCAL. With MULTISCALE, a data analyst may, for example, wish to see if an unconstrained solution fits better than a corresponding constrained solution (e.g., fitting the IDIOSCAL versus the INDSCAL models to the same input data in the same dimensionality), or test whether increasing the dimensionality of a solution leads to significantly improved fit. The user may also place linear constraints on the coordinates (X) fitted for the objects.

In many ways, the most novel contribution embodied in MULTISCALE is the plotting of ellipsoidal confidence regions for the object coordinates and (in principle) for the source weights. These regions can be very helpful for showing which objects or groups of objects can be regarded as truly distinct in the object space. Examples of such MULTISCALE analyses appear in Chapter 10 of Schiffman et al. (1981). Regions for the sources can be used for similar purposes, but we predict that such regions should be interpreted with more caution than in the case of object coordinates.

Weinberg, Carroll, and Cohen (1984) used bootstrap (Efron, 1982) and jackknife (Tukey, 1958; R. G. Miller, 1974) techniques and employed the SINDSCAL (Pruzansky, 1975) program to obtain confidence regions for both simulated and real data sets. This approach entailed much more labor but considerably weaker assumptions about the data than would the use of MULTISCALE. Figure 10 shows a comparison of confidence regions derived using the approach of Weinberg et al. (1984) versus that of Ramsay's MULTISCALE.

ALSCAL

The ALSCAL (for Alternating Least Squares SCALing) program of Takane et al. (1977) can be used either for two-way MDS (as discussed in Kruskal and Wish, 1978) or for fitting the three-way IDIOSCAL and INDSCAL models (Carroll and Chang, 1970, 1972). (Appendix D provides a summary of the technical details.) In the last instance, ALSCAL is, like Ramsay's MULTISCALE, an alternative to Pruzansky's SINDSCAL program for fitting the INDSCAL model. As with MULTISCALE, ALSCAL has a provision (lacking in SINDSCAL) for missing data, but the implementation in releases prior to ALSCAL·4 may pose a hazard for the unwary user: all input data values less than or equal to zero are treated as missing. Thus, if the observed data include zeros or negative values (e.g., correlations), it is first necessary to transform the data (e.g., by adding a positive constant) before entering them into the ALSCAL program.

A distinctive innovation of the ALSCAL program is that, unlike SINDSCAL and MULTISCALE, it allows the user to declare explicitly that the data are from scale types other than interval. Not surprisingly, nominal scale data can lead to precarious results (see Young and Null, 1978, for two-way MDS results). Schiffman et al. (1981, p. 171) recommend against declaring data to be of ratio scale quality and suggest that most proximity data are probably ordinal. Hahn, Widaman, and MacCallum (1978) concluded that under most conditions, the INDSCAL program (Chang and Carroll, 1969), despite its assumption of interval scale data, recovered structure in ordinal data better than did the ordinal version of ALSCAL.

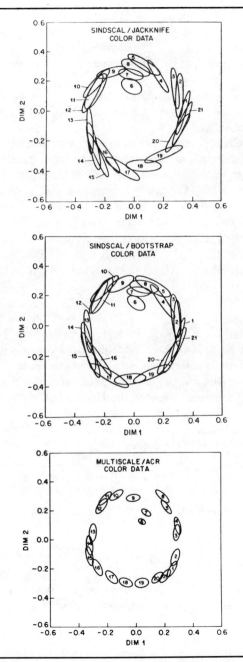

Figure 10: Confidence regions for object spaces resulting from SINDSCAL and MULTISCALE analyses of the same data. (Reproduced with permission from Weinberg, Carroll, and Cohen, 1984.)

Although the original article (Takane et al., 1977) announcing the ALSCAL algorithm emphasized that it included options for matrix conditional (as in SINDSCAL and MULTISCALE) as well as matrix unconditional analyses, the latter innovation has empirically shown little, if any, advantage for analyses fitting the INDSCAL model. Schiffman et al. (1981, p. 175) give an unqualified recommendation of declaring data to be matrix conditional when fitting the INDSCAL model with ALSCAL.

The ALSCAL program fits the object coordinates (X) and source weights (W) without first transforming the input proximity data to be scalar products, as required in the SINDSCAL program (see Appendix B). Because ALSCAL uses a measure of badness-of-fit called SSTRESS (not easily related to the VAF measure used in INDSCAL and SINDSCAL) and employs the *square* of the recovered distances $d_{ij,k}$ in the optimization procedures, its solutions can and often do differ from those found by MULTISCALE and SINDSCAL for the same data set. Examples of ALSCAL analyses are given in Chapter 9 of Schiffman et al. (1981).

TUCKALS3

Three-mode, three-way MDS represents Ledyard Tucker's (1972) application of his (1964) three-mode principal components analysis to a matrix of derived scalar products, so as to obtain an "individual differences" (among sources of data) MDS analysis. Explication of the current model requires review of the IDIOSCAL model given above in equation [5]. Specifically, in the model that Kroonenberg and de Leeuw (1980) have labeled "Tucker3," matrix C_k from equation [5] is now assumed to be of the form

$$C_k = \sum_{s=1}^{S} a_{ks} G_s \qquad [6]$$

where G_s is the s-th "basis" matrix. The preceding equation can be expanded:

$$c_{rr'k} = \sum_{s=1}^{S} a_{ks} g_{srr'}, \qquad [7]$$

where $A \equiv \{a_{ks}\}$ is the S-dimensional source space in the three-mode scaling model, while $g_{srr'}$ is an element in the "core matrix," sometimes called the "core box," since it is actually a three-way $S \times R \times R$ array. Here, the symmetric $R \times R$ matrix C_k, defining a "quadratic form" specifying the generalized Euclidean metric for source k, can be viewed as a linear combination of S "basic" (symmetric) matrices G_s ($s = 1 \cdots S$). The coordinates for source k in the Tucker3 source space, a_{ks}, define the coefficients of the linear combination for source k.

The TUCKALS3 (Kroonenberg and de Leeuw, 1980) program for fitting this model should not be regarded as an alternative to any of the others discussed in this paper. Tucker's (1972) approach to three-way MDS is *sui generis*, and so are the solutions and interpretations resulting from such a program as TUCKALS3 for fitting it. Several features of such scaling representations should be noted (Carroll and Wish, 1974a). First, the orientation of neither the object space nor the source space is unique. Second, the source space and the object space may have different dimensionalities for the same data (S and R, respectively). This feature of Tucker's approach to three-way MDS provides considerably more flexibility than does the INDSCAL model. Third, in addition to providing coordinates (X) for the objects and weights (W) for the sources, fitting Tucker's model also yields a "core matrix" or "core box" (the three-way array containing the elements $g_{srr'}$ of equation [7]). Given appropriate transformations (allowable in Tucker's model) of the object and source spaces, followed by the corresponding "companion" transformations of this "core box," it is possible to interpret the matrices G_s corresponding to two-way slices of the core box as matrices of correlations among the dimensions of the object space (and/or as defining rotations and possible reweightings of rotated dimensions) for a set of "idealized individuals" in an interpretation using the points-of-view (Tucker and Messick, 1963) approach discussed earlier. (See Tucker, 1972, for a detailed discussion.)

The TUCKALS3 program assumes interval scale input data, but as Kroonenberg and de Leeuw (1980, p. 91) note, their program could be modified to accept data from other scale types. Because this program allows fitting a model that is explicitly both three-way and three-mode, the concept of symmetry within each source's matrix is not necessarily relevant. Thus, in analyzing the Miller and Nicely (1955) data, Kroonenberg and de Leeuw (1980, pp. 79-90) did not have to symmetrize conjugate off-diagonal entries, as in the analyses reported above (details are given in the Appendix of Arabie and Soli, 1982). That is, the TUCKALS3 analysis allowed Kroonenberg and de Leeuw (1980) to treat stimuli (the signals that came through the observers' earphones) and responses (what the observers reported hearing afterward) as two separate modes, unlike the symmetrization required above that implicitly equated these two modes.

This approach entails a model which differs from that given in equation [5] in two important respects. First, the model assumes the data (confusions in this case) are linear with *squared* distances rather than first power distances as assumed in the standard form of the (metric) IDIOSCAL model in equation [5]. Most importantly, since the analysis Kroonenberg and de Leeuw report was on the nonsymmetrized confusions, the model for distances was also a nonsymmetric model. The particular nonsymmetric model assumed can be specified by replacing the values in the second term in parentheses on the right side of equation [5] with a second set of parameters (say x^*) which are not necessarily the same as the x values. In their actual analysis of the confusions data, however, Kroonenberg and de Leeuw found that the two sets of parameters (the x and the x^* values) were very nearly equal after appropriate rotation, and could thus be set equal with very little deterioration in goodness-of-fit. Therefore, those authors concluded that "symmetrization does not really violate the structure of the [Miller-Nicely] data" (1980, p. 83). For the case of symmetric input data, the model Kroonenberg and de Leeuw used for the distances reduces to that given in equation [5], except with the special structure on C_k defined in equations [6] and [7] while, in this symmetric case, both the matrices G_s $[s = 1 \cdots S]$ and C_k $[k = 1 \cdots K]$ can be assumed symmetric as well.

Kroonenberg and de Leeuw also analyzed the Miller-Nicely data as just described but with another method they call TUCKALS2. In the symmetric case TUCKALS2 assumes a generalized Euclidean distance of the form given in equation [5] but *without* the constraints on the G_s matrices imposed in equations [6] and [7]. In the nonsymmetric case the method fits the (nonsymmetric) model for distances discussed earlier (with x^* values replacing x values in the second expression in parentheses on the right side of equation [5]), also without constraints on the G_s matrices. Kroonenberg and de Leeuw report that they obtained very similar results whether they used the TUCKALS2 analysis (with no constraints on the G_s matrices) or the TUCKALS3 analysis (*with* such constraints). The TUCKALS2 analysis, because it also showed no marked deviation from symmetry, was nearly equivalent to an IDIOSCAL analysis (except for the assumption of linearity of the data with *squared* rather than *first* power distances). However, the authors report using a procedure that rotated the object (consonant phoneme) coordinates so that the G matrices were very nearly diagonal, which is the form of G matrices making the IDIOSCAL model equivalent to INDSCAL (with the diagonal entries then corresponding to the source weights). Furthermore, Kroonenberg and de Leeuw report that, after this rotation effecting near diagonality of the G matrices, the interpretation of the stimulus dimensions was considerably improved. This finding is consistent with the assumption that the INDSCAL model in equation [2], rather than the more general IDIOSCAL model in equation [5], is probably sufficient for these data (in addition to the advantages in uniqueness of orientation and interpretability afforded by the INDSCAL model).

The first decade after the invention of Tucker's model, which can be viewed even more generally as a three-mode components or factor analytic model, saw relatively few applications, but in more recent years the number has grown dramatically, and such algorithmic developments and improvements as the least-squares program TUCKALS3 (Kroonenberg and de Leeuw, 1980) have undoubtedly contributed to the model's increased popularity. (See related developments by Bentler and Lee, 1978, 1979, Kroonenberg, Lammers, and Stoop, 1985, and the chapters in Law, Snyder, Hattie, and McDonald, 1984, by Bloxom, 1984, Harshman and Lundy, 1984, and by other contributors.) Kroonenberg (1983) has provided a detailed bibliography of developments in this area of three-way data analysis.

6. THREE-WAY ("INDIVIDUAL DIFFERENCES") CLUSTERING

The models and associated computer programs covered thus far in our paper have all assumed a continuous spatial representation. Shepard (1972a, 1972b) was among the earliest to emphasize that such discrete methods of data analysis as clustering can often be used profitably in conjunction with spatial MDS models, to bring out complementary aspects of structure underlying the data. The term "complementary" bears emphasizing because we do not see either MDS or clustering models being inherently superior to the other or necessarily being closer to some (generally unknowable) "true" underlying structure.

An elegant result by Holman (1972) showed that "error-free" two-way proximity data corresponding to objects in a low-dimensional Euclidean space are incompatible with the ultrametric inequality that characterizes most commonly used methods of hierarchical clustering (see Hubert, 1974; Hartigan, 1975; Murtagh, 1985). Concisely, proximity data perfectly satisfying the ultrametric inequality require a Euclidean space of very high dimensionality (so high that the space cannot be interpreted) if a good fit is to be achieved. In other words, data can satisfy either the Euclidean spatial model without error in a low dimensionality or the ultrametric clustering model without error, but not both models simultaneously. However, Kruskal (1977) noted that it is empirically the case for *real* proximity data that good fits to one of the two models are usually concomitant with good fits to the other, and that complementary interpretations are often found for such data sets. (Such interpretations often show convex contours enveloping each cluster's constituent objects, which are also embedded in an MDS spatial solution. To date, however, there is no analytical demonstration to support the common expectation of convex clusters for either hierarchical or ADCLUS / INDCLUS clustering.)

It is our strong recommendation that MDS analyses be accompanied by cluster analyses and vice versa whenever the data permit. Furthermore, there is a corollary to this recommendation: performing a legitimate cluster analysis requires using a method that explicitly and objectively seeks clusters. One should *not* try visually to "define" clusters on the basis of a spatial representation of the objects resulting from an analysis based on such continuous models as principal components analysis, factor analysis, or spatial MDS. It is of course natural to refer to groupings and other spatial patterns in such a configuration of objects, but to elevate such subjective groupings to the status of "clusters" and suggest that they have any reality other than visual is misleading.

This practice of visual, subjective clustering dates back to the factor analytic tradition and an era when computation was generally done manually and much less was known about models for data analysis. Independent results from Ling (1971) and Baker and Hubert (1976, p. 877) cast doubt on the existence (statistically defined) of "clusters" in the prototypical demonstration (Harman, 1976). More recent results by W. C. Chang (1983) have further demonstrated that using principal components analysis for reducing the nominal dimensions of data prior to applying a method of clustering is an unwise practice. By extension, the same warning applies to using MDS for such "reduction" of data prior to clustering. The latter technique should be given its own chance to find structure in data, without impedance from such misguided "reduction."

In summary, we can think of only three excuses for committing "visual clustering": (a) the data analyst has consulted an out-of-date reference on clustering, (b) computational laziness, or (c) the number of objects is very large (e.g., several hundred). Since principal components and factor analysis can be run relatively fast on much larger data sets than is the case for most combinatorial clustering algorithms, it may not be feasible to run a proper cluster analysis in such situations.

CHOOSING A METHOD OF CLUSTERING

For two-way data matrices that are either two-mode or one-mode, there are many different methods of clustering (Hubert, 1974; Hartigan, 1975; also see recent issues of *Journal of Classification* and *Psychometrika*). Since the focus of this paper is three-way data, the method of clustering emphasized here (the INDCLUS model and algorithm of Carroll and Arabie, 1979, 1982, 1983) is one explicitly designed for such data. (Also, the details of the algorithm have been published and an exportable computer program is, at the time this paper is written, distributed by AT&T Bell Laboratories.)

Kroonenberg and de Leeuw (1980, p. 83) in their analysis (discussed above) of the Miller-Nicely data noted the absence of a three-way clustering method to complement their (three-way) TUCKALS3 analysis. Similarly, although Rosenberg and Kim (1975) obtained a three-way MDS representation (presented above) of their kinship terms by fitting the INDSCAL model, those authors had to perform separate (two-way) hierarchical cluster analyses on various subsets of their data because no three-way clustering method was available. (See the Introduction of this monograph for a discussion of the disadvantages of performing K separate two-way analyses, in contrast to an overall three-way analysis.) Knoke (1983, p. 1071) noted the absence of an adequate model for three-way data on social networks. The INDCLUS (for INdividual Differences CLUStering) model and algorithm of Carroll and Arabie (1983; Carroll, 1975) was developed to meet this perceived need. Like the INDSCAL model, however, INDCLUS is most easily explained by beginning with the two-way case.

THE (TWO-WAY) ADCLUS MODEL FOR OVERLAPPING, NONHIERARCHICAL CLUSTERING

Shepard and Arabie (1979; Arabie and Shepard, 1973) devised an approach to clustering that began with a substantive model (rather than with a convenient algorithm, as in traditional approaches to hierarchical clustering) that posited the observed similarity (more generally, proximity) between a pair of objects to be an additive function based on a set of R relevant "features" (cf. Tversky, 1977), represented as clusters (i.e., subsets) of the set of objects under study. [These clusters are allowed — but not required — to overlap, in contrast to (a) hierarchical clustering, where the only admissible form of overlap is nesting and (b) partitioning, where no overlap is permitted.] That is, a set of features, represented as clusters, was to be found, as well as associated numerical weights, such that the sum of the weights of all clusters containing a given pair of objects would reconstruct or predict the input proximity value that pair and similarly for all the $I(I-1)/2$ distinct pairs of objects from the set of I objects.

Formally, the ADCLUS (for ADditive CLUStering) model of Shepard and Arabie predicts interobject similarity as

$$s_{ij} \cong \sum_{r=1}^{R} w_r p_{ir} p_{jr} + c, \qquad [8]$$

where w_r is the numerical weight (assumed to be nonnegative) of the r-th cluster $(r = 1 \cdots R)$; p_{ir} is unity if object i $(i = 1 \cdots I)$ is present in cluster r, otherwise zero, and similarly for p_{jr} and object j. The additive constant c can alternatively be represented as the weight (not assumed to be nonnegative) of an $(R + 1)$-st "universal" cluster comprising the complete set of the I objects. The weights in the ADCLUS model gauge the salience of their associated clusters, just as weights do for dimensions in the INDSCAL model. With the exception of the additive constant c, negative weights are as substantively meaningless in the ADCLUS model as they were for INDSCAL. Fitting the additive constant is required by the mechanics of linear regression so that VAF can be computed as the measure of goodness-of-fit, and is particularly appropriate when the data are measured at best on an interval scale.

The following qualifications to the preceding variables should be noted. The input data are assumed to be the $I(I-1)/2$ entries constituting a two-way symmetric (or symmetrized) proximity matrix having no missing entries. Although the raw data may be in the form of either similarities or dissimilarities, they are first transformed linearly into similarities. (Since the data are assumed to be on an interval scale, the particular transformation chosen in no way affects the goodness-of-fit, but does allow for the standardization of various parameters described below.) $\mathbf{S} \equiv \{s_{ij}\}$ will always refer to these transformed proximities, to which the fitted $\hat{\mathbf{S}}$ matrix is being compared. Turning to the $\mathbf{P} \equiv \{p_{ir}\}$ matrix, note that each column represents one of the R subsets (or clusters — we use the terms interchangeably here), with the ones of that column defining constituency of objects within the respective subset. Thus, fitting the (two-way) ADCLUS model entails simultaneously fitting a set of clusters (**P**) and their associated weights (**W**) to one input proximity matrix. Again, we would like to emphasize that the model *per se* imposes no constraints on the patterns of overlap that may emerge among the clusters when the model is fitted to data. Partitioning (in which case the clusters are mutually exclusive and exhaustive vis-à-vis the set of objects) and hierarchical clustering are subsumed as special cases of the ADCLUS model, albeit ones that have yet to arise empirically for real data.

Shepard and Arabie (1979) provided illustrative applications of fitting this model to several types of data, and readers unfamiliar with the two-way model may wish to refer to that paper. In addition, those authors devised an algorithm and associated program, also called ADCLUS, for fitting the model. That program, which is now mainly of historical interest, sought only certain kinds of clusters (suggested by complete-link hierarchical clustering) and thus provided what might be viewed as constrained solutions of the ADCLUS model. Corter and Tversky's (1986) EXTREE (for EXtended TREE) approach to clustering is based on yet another constrained form of the ADCLUS model, which also extends that model by including "distinctive features" (specific to distinct objects) as well as the "common features" corresponding to clusters or subsets in the ADCLUS model.

A general-purpose and exportable program called MAPCLUS (for MAthematical Programming CLUStering) was devised by Arabie and Carroll (1980a, 1980b) for fitting the (two-way) ADCLUS model, and this program supplanted the earlier program Shepard and Arabie (1979) had called ADCLUS.

Examples of using the MAPCLUS program for fitting the two-way case of the ADCLUS model have appeared by Arabie and Carroll (1980b, 1987), Arabie, Carroll, DeSarbo, and Wind (1981), Eckes (1981, 1981/1982), Purcell (1984), Rabin and Frank (1982), and Shepard and Arabie (1979). Another application, using the SAS statistical package to fit the ADCLUS model, appears in Srivastava, Alpert, and Shocker (1984). (Since the algorithm used in SAS to fit the model has not been published, it will not be considered in this paper.) DeSarbo (1982) has provided a generalization (GENNCLUS) of the ADCLUS model to the case of two-way two-mode data. Several of these papers observed that further information about individual differences in weighting of the clusters would be of interest.

INDCLUS: A CLUSTERING COUNTERPART TO INDSCAL

Recall that the input data for such programs as Pruzansky's (1975) SINDSCAL for fitting the INDSCAL model consisted of a set of symmetric proximity matrices Δ_k, $k = 1 \cdots K$. Since the (two-way) ADCLUS model and its (three-way) generalization INDCLUS are both discussed more easily if we consider the input data to be similarities, we will now switch to using S_k ($k = 1 \cdots K$) to denote the input proximity data. (As noted in the discussion of the ADCLUS model, if the raw data were dissimilarities, then they are first linearly transformed to be similarities.) Just as INDSCAL assumed a common set of R dimensions for all K sources of data, INDCLUS assumes a common set of R clusters, whose numerical weights vary as a joint function of which cluster and source of data are being considered. (One way of interpreting these clusters is as dimensions in a space not necessarily Euclidean, with the objects having coordinates required to

be binary to indicate presence or absence in the corresponding cluster.)
The INDCLUS model is written

$$s_{ij,k} \cong \sum_{r=1}^{R} w_{kr} p_{ir} p_{jr} + c_k \qquad [9]$$

where $s_{ij,k}$ is the similarity between objects i and j for source k ($k = 1 \cdots K$), w_{kr} is the weight for source k on cluster r, and c_k (*not related to the variable by the same name used in equations [6] and [7]*) is the additive constant for source k. Thus, we have generalized the ADCLUS model in equation [9] so as to fit a series of K proximities matrices. All K subjects, conditions, or whatever the sources of data happen to be, have the same set of clusters, defined by the unities in each of the R columns of **P**. (The additive constants c_k and, of course, the other weights vary over sources.)

While the ADCLUS model is formulated in terms of similarities rather than of dissimilarities, and superficially has the form of a *scalar product* rather than a *distance* model, it is possible to reformulate ADCLUS as a (non-Euclidean) distance model by the simple device of subtracting the similarity values (and thus the similarities predicted by the ADCLUS or INDCLUS model) from a constant (sufficiently large enough, on the "model" or right side of equation [8], to guarantee satisfaction of the triangle inequality). (In the case of INDCLUS, a different such constant might be introduced for each source.) The resulting "metric" is of the form **C** (or $\mathbf{C}_k$ in the INDCLUS case) minus a weighted count of common features (clusters) for each pair of objects. Since this constant is (conceptually) added to (the negative of) *both* sides of equations [8] or [9] respectively, we obviously can (conceptually) *subtract* that constant (or those constants) from both sides and then multiply by -1, resulting in the (equivalent) versions of the ADCLUS or INDCLUS models given in [8] or [9].

While this conversion from an apparent scalar product to an apparent distance formulation of these models may seem at first only a fairly vacuous intellectual exercise, there in fact is one noteworthy implication: in the case when the clusters are *nested*, consistent with a tree structure (that is, every pair of distinct clusters is either *disjoint* or one contains the other as a proper subset), then the metric induced by the operation of subtracting the (model) similarities from a sufficiently large constant turns out to be an ultrametric (see Hartigan, 1967; Jardine, Jardine, and Sibson, 1967; Johnson, 1967), which characterizes the tree structures most commonly derived in *hierarchical* clustering.

FITTING THE INDCLUS MODEL

Just as the INDCLUS model is a three-way generalization of the ADCLUS model, the INDCLUS program (Carroll and Arabie, 1982) is a generalization of the MAPCLUS (Arabie and Carroll, 1980b) program for fitting the ADCLUS model. In fact, when one specifies that there is $K = 1$ input proximity matrix for the INDCLUS program, the resulting analysis is generally the same result the user would get from using the (two-way) MAPCLUS program.

The MAPCLUS and INDCLUS programs both have two phases. Since a detailed technical account is given in Arabie and Carroll (1980a, 1980b) and Carroll and Arabie (1982, 1983), we present only a cursory overview in the present paper. The first phase combines a "mathematical programming" technique with alternating least squares. Concretely, we begin by allowing the entries in the **P** matrix (which defines the cluster structure) of equation [9] to vary *continuously* even though the final solution requires that they be binary (i.e., having only values of zero or one) for the discrete, additive model to be fitted. The mathematical programming technique causes the entries to be asymptotically binary. The alternating least squares framework uses "major" iterations which consist of round-robin efforts at fitting in turn each subset (i.e., cluster) and its associated weights for each of the K sources of data, using the residuals (i.e., the part of the data not fitted earlier) computed from the other subsets. (These iterations are called "major" because they are at the highest level of nesting of the various types of iterations used in the programs.) Thus, the iterative procedure seeks approximately to maximize the VAF in each of the input proximity matrices, subject to producing binary entries in the **P** matrix.

When those entries are sufficiently close to zero or one, the program "polishes" or rounds them off so that they are exactly binary, and a first (discrete) solution has been found. Then a somewhat counter-intuitive ("*de novo*") strategy commences: We "zero out" both the fitted weight and cluster and re-estimate them both for each subset in turn using the same approach the program uses to produce a rational initial configuration. Further details are given in Arabie and Carroll (1980a). Even though the VAF sometimes drops slightly on the first *de novo* major iteration, VAF generally tends to recover in succeeding *de novo* iterations, often to a higher value than before the start of the *de novo* iterations. When improvement in VAF becomes negligible, the *de novo* iterations are terminated.

In summary, the first phase consists of: (a) "pre-polishing" major iterations during which the entries of **P** are not yet binary, (b) a first iteration of polishing, and (c) further iterations of polishing, via the *de novo* approach. Note that only (b) and (c) produce discrete solutions to the INDCLUS model of equation [9].

The second phase of the INDCLUS program consists of two alternating approaches to combinatorial optimization. In the first or "doubleton" strategy, we consider reversing the membership status of each of the $I(I-1)/2$ pairs of objects for the first cluster. The change (if one exists) that would lead to the greatest increase in VAF is made (unless it would cause any of the clusters' weights to become negative), and then the process is repeated on the first cluster until no further improvements are found. For example, in the first cluster of Table 7 below, based on the Rosenberg and Kim (1975) data, we would consider the pair (aunt, brother). Because the first kinship term currently does not belong and the second does, our tentative new cluster becomes (aunt, father, grandfather, grandson, nephew, son, uncle). Not surprisingly, this particular doubleton change was not advantageous!

After finishing the doubleton strategy on the first cluster, we proceed to do the same with each of the remaining $R-1$ clusters in turn. Then, we shift to the singleton strategy which simply considers reversing the membership status of the I *single* entries in the first cluster, so that, for example, (aunt) is tentatively appended to the first cluster. The strategy is implemented within and over clusters just as with the doubleton strategy described earlier. When a consecutive overall loop of these two strategies has failed to increase VAF or (much less likely) 15 iterations of the two strategies have been carried out, the process is terminated.

The two phases are summarized in Table 5, and an INDCLUS analysis can, at the user's option, begin at any of the four stages listed in that Table, starting at Stage A as the default. The second phase (combinatorial optimization, Stage D) has far fewer control parameters than does the first (Stages A, B, and C) so that it proceeds more or less automatically. The user is allowed to define values for many of the control parameters in phase one (discussed below and, in much greater detail, in Carroll and Arabie, 1982), but we suspect most readers will be content to use the default values.

There is, however, one option meriting comment. Specifically, the (two-way) MAPCLUS program has no option to constrain the clusters' weights to be nonnegative (so they will not be uninterpretable), because we empirically found few negative weights during data analyses. On the other hand, early computational experience in developing INDCLUS showed that, with so many more weights typically being estimated in the three-way case, negative values can be a problem, and Carroll and Arabie (1983, p. 161) therefore included an option for the user to require the weights to be nonnegative. (Just as in MAPCLUS,

TABLE 5

Overview of Iterative Structure of INDCLUS

[A] Pre-polishing major iterations
(maximum number of such iterations = ITPRE)

[B] One major iteration of polishing

[C] Further major (*de novo*) iterations of polishing, with estimation of weights and subsets begun anew

Note: The maximum number of iterations (ITPRE for [A], + 1 for [B], + the number for [C]) = M15, as declared by the user.

[D] Combinatorial optimization (upper limit of 15 iterations)

the default is not to constrain the weights.) Since MAPCLUS does not have this option, a user with only one input proximity matrix who wishes to constrain the weights to be nonnegative would have to declare $K = 1$ and use INDCLUS for this two-way analysis. Otherwise, it will always be computationally more efficient to use MAPCLUS rather than INDCLUS for $K = 1$.

EXAMPLE: ROSENBERG AND KIM'S (1975) DATA

We have already described the sorting experiment conducted by Rosenberg and Kim. The six matrices listed below in Table 6 (without the additional pre-processing used for fitting the data to the INDSCAL model) served as input for an INDCLUS analysis. (Because the details of setting up an analysis similar to this one are available in Carroll and Arabie [1982, pp. 24-30 and the Appendix], the following discussion will not repeat such details.) Empirically, a practice has developed of expecting at most $I/2$ clusters as an upper bound and then decreasing that number until the fit is no longer acceptable to the user. One diagnostic of too few clusters is when highly interpretable clusters previously obtained are either lost or merged into large and less interpretable amalgams. Solutions with seven, six ... three clusters were obtained in the present analysis, and a five-cluster solution seemed to provide the best tradeoff between interpretability and goodness-of-fit.

Table 7 presents a five-cluster solution from an INDCLUS analysis of the six matrices (matrix unconditional analysis), with 81.1% of the variance accounted for (over all six matrices). The clusters are easily interpreted. In the order listed, the first two are sex-defined, the third is the collateral relatives, the fourth is the nuclear family, and the fifth consists of grandparents and grandchildren. The patterns of the weights also yield interesting results. For example, the statement of

TABLE 6

Rosenberg and Kim (1975) Data for INDCLUS Analysis

```
005  0  5  0 15  0  1  2 17
000000000000000000000000000000000000000000000000000000000000000000000000
   0   0   0   0
```

BLANK
BLANK

```
ROSENBERG-KIM 1975 S-MEAS FOR FEMALE,MALE MULT SORTS1,2,+SINGLE SORT
   6 115  1  1
(15F2.0)
```

79	1
5670	2
366671	3
76227863	4
3473702577	5
763575763261	6
36787534761748	7
7727717131491763	8
336876155031763077	9
57335574387437783080	10
1375543279317738733945	11
384870206728773474217735	12
77207248167035772662327266	13
4738597932783777357513577938	14
76	1
5563	2
605673	3
70427852	4
5774724478	5
725876764557	6
54797852702929	7
7454706855283056	8
526480242954704577	9
51524872617159785380	10
2671495380527859706126	11
582365346553795873437152	12
77357128256853754651547155	13
2856547750775574596926527559	14
78	1
5362	2
546671	3
73337263	4
5274754974	5
755270734852	6
48777652732731	7
7848697250302552	8
456077363150744776	9
58484572547451764780	10
3075524977497552745330	11
513269426149775275347447	12
78416728367251744763477467	13
3151477746774875517429577853	14
74	1
6056	2
545767	3
66366862	4
5169653478	5
685369743962	6
43787447693431	7
7445616750343562	8
406274333250683976	9
64414567526549753978	10

TABLE 6 (Continued)

386751418039754 9665330	11
5231622763407 75169366840	12
7832633534684 9773763406757	13
28505479407644695 16639637753	14
83	1
3877	2
796183	3
79558443	4
7982826983	5
847684837348	6
78838474823811	7
8573818074133848	8
726384341374827383	9
49745381778078847383	10
428353748572857979797912	11
7710785263738376825581 76	12
855282143480748369437481 61	13
10773985728578847979 42498379	14
84	1
5573	2
716780	3
76428261	4
7177795582	5
846981816660	6
70828265804621	7
8560797366214361	8
635983441966816382	9
596958797279718 56485	10
458259648563847 2807220	11
72217547615983687 6468267	12
84498022447565815660658064	13
17715584638570847 27646608470	14

AUNTBROTHRCOUSINDAUGHTFATHERGRDAUGGRFATHGRMOTH GRSONMOTHERNEPHEW NIECE
SISTER   SON UNCLE
SMEAF1SMEAF2SMEAM1SMEAM2SME1SFSME1SM

Rosenberg and Kim (1975, p. 489) that subjects restricted to a single-sort ignore sex as a basis of organization is strongly supported by the relatively low weights for the sex-defined clusters in the first two columns (especially for female subjects) of Table 7. For the multiple-sort conditions, it is interesting to note that female subjects emphasized sex in the first sorting (given that the two relevant clusters have much higher weights), whereas male subjects waited until the second sorting to emphasize sex as a basis for sorting the kinship terms. Across all conditions, females' data were better fitted to the model than were males' data. Also, data from the first sort were better fitted than for the second sort, both for females and males. (Further details of the analysis are given in Carroll and Arabie, 1983, pp. 162-166.)

Other published applications of the INDCLUS model include cognitive development of children's arithmetical abilities (K. Miller and Gelman, 1983), U.S. Supreme Court decisions (Carroll and Arabie, 1983), and the three-way Miller-Nicely data (Soli, Arabie and Carroll, 1986).

TABLE 7

INDCLUS Solution (Matrix Unconditional) for Kinship Data
from Rosenberg and Kim (1975)

Weights for Different Sources of Data

Females' Single-Sort	Males' Single-Sort	Females' First Sort	Females' Second Sort	Males' First Sort	Males' Second Sort	Elements of Subset	Interpretation
.052	.143	.551	.241	.299	.295	brother, father, grandfather, grandson, nephew, son, uncle	Male relatives, excluding cousin
.049	.146	.554	.246	.291	.306	aunt, daughter, granddaughter, grandmother, mother, niece, sister	Female relatives, excluding cousin
.552	.397	.283	.373	.340	.237	aunt, cousin, nephew, niece, uncle	Collateral (Romney & D'Andrade, 1964) relatives
.478	.372	.206	.322	.241	.219	brother, daughter, father, mother, sister, son	Nuclear family
.626	.449	.251	.385	.395	.253	granddaughter, grandfather, grandmother, grandson	Direct ancestors and descendants ±2 generations removed
.055	.075	.132	.158	.158	.207	Additive constants	
78.6%	68.8%	96.3%	78.9%	82.4%	71.7%	Variance accounted within condition	Overall VAF = 81.1%

FUTURE PROSPECTS

In addition to the developments for three-way clustering discussed by Carroll and Arabie (1983, pp. 166-167), the relevant journals in this area continue to publish new models and algorithms for three-way analyses, using clustering and/or scaling (e.g., Carroll, Clark, and DeSarbo, 1984; DeSarbo and Carroll, 1985; Bieber, 1986).

7. SOFTWARE FOR THREE-WAY MDS

Table 8 lists sources for some of the computer programs discussed in this paper. Additional information and addresses are given in Kruskal and Wish (1978, pp. 78-82).

TABLE 8

Sources for MDS Software

SINDSCAL, INDSCAL, INDCLUS, PREFMAP3:
    Computing Information Service
    Room 2F-128A
    AT&T Bell Laboratories
    600 Mountain Avenue
    Murray Hill, NJ 07974
    USA

MULTISCALE:
    International Educational Services
    P.O. Box 536
    Mooresville, IN 46158
    USA

TUCKALS2 and TUCKALS3:
    Dr. Pieter M. Kroonenberg
    Vakgroep Wijsgerige en Empirische Pedagogiek
    Subfaculteit der P.A.W.
    Rijksuniversiteit Leiden
    Stationsplein 10-12
    2312 AK Leiden
    The Netherlands

PARAFAC:
    Scientific Software Associates
    48 Wilson Avenue
    London, Ontario, Canada N6H 1X3

ALSCAL:
    Professor Forrest W. Young
    Psychometric Laboratory
    University of North Carolina
    Chapel Hill, NC 27514
    USA

NOTE: Neither the authors nor the publishers of this book assume responsibility for the distribution or accuracy of the software listed here.

Although we have discussed the programs without specifying computers on which they run, we have generally assumed the availability of sizable mainframes supporting large FORTRAN programs. Nonetheless, we have found that several of the programs are easily adapted to such personal computers as the IBM XT, IBM AT, and AT&T UNIX PC, but that the amount of time required for analyses is often very long. We expect this situation to improve as newer machines become available.

APPENDIX A

Control Parameters for a SINDSCAL Analysis of Miller-Nicely Data

For various substantive reasons, INDSCAL solutions in dimensionalities of six, five ... two were sought for the transformed data. Table A.1 lists the first several lines (more generally, "records" or "card images" on disk) of input to the SINDSCAL program. (We will refer to "control cards" or "parameter cards" even though we realize most users will have records on disk files rather than punched cards as an input medium.)

The discussion below gives a detailed description of setting up the input deck for running the SINDSCAL program. In the present discussion of Table A.1, we cover only the values of control parameters used to analyze the Miller-Nicely (1955) data. The first record gives the numerical values of four input parameters: MAXDIM, MINDIM, NMAT, NSTIM. The first parameter specifies the maximum dimensionality for which a spatial solution is sought, and the second gives the minimum dimensionality. In the present analysis, a solution will first be computed in a six-dimensional space, then five- and so on, until a two-dimensional solution completes the set of analyses for the three-way Miller-Nicely data set. NMAT ("number of matrices") corresponds to K, the number of sources (17 experimental conditions), and NSTIM ("number of stimuli") to I, the number of objects (16 consonant phonemes). These four parameters for controlling the execution of SINDSCAL are entered as integers (without decimal points), right-justified in fields of four columns' width. Thus, the successive values end in columns 4, 8, 12, and 16. This FORTRAN format is referred to as (4I4) since there are four integer fields, with each being four columns wide.

The second record (or "card image") contains five more input parameters: ITMAX, IRDATA, IPUNCH, IPLOT, and IRN, in (5I4) format, so that fields end in columns 4, 8, 12, 16, and 20. The first parameter refers to the maximum number of iterations the user wishes to allow the SINDSCAL program in fitting the INDSCAL model. The second, IRDATA, specifies the shape and type of the input data matrices (assumed to be uniform over all K matrices). The allowable shapes are triangular lower halfmatrix (with or without the principal diagonal) or full (square) $I \times I$ matrices, and the types comprise similarities, dissimilarities, Euclidean distances, covariances, and product-moment correlations. Although the nine options of IRDATA are listed below, three points are worth noting: (a) regardless of whether self-similarities (i.e, the diagonal entitles) are read in, they are not used (except in the case of covariances; see discussion below) in fitting the INDSCAL model, (b) if a full matrix option is specified and nonsymmetry is present, only one entry (arbitrarily chosen) from each of the unequal conjugate pairs is used, and (c) there is no provision for missing data. Elaborating on the last point, the best procedure is for the user to supply estimates for missing data. It is crucial that some value be entered even if it is only blanks that the program will read as zeros.

66

TABLE A.1

Beginning of Input Data for SINDSCAL Analysis of
Log-Transformed Data from Miller and Nicely (1955)

```
  6    2   17   16
 50    1   -1    0  600
SINDSCAL ANALYSIS OF 3-WAY LOG TRANSFORMED MILLER-NICELY (1955) DATA
(10F8.5)
  .03181
  .04387 -.06500
  .13111 -.12142 -.04837
  .16116 -.09372 -.08539 -.16418
  .05839 -.12744  .06318 -.28092  .03515
  .03036 -.07007  .01170 -.13626 -.06394  .18862
 -.14783 -.44249 -.23336 -.14002 -.07201 -.23747 -.23665
 -.08539 -.17542 -.22709 -.16210 -.05750 -.07119 -.04653 -.06646
  .13501
 -.09055 -.19812 -.18006 -.28175 -.14783 -.16571 -.36311 -.10336 -.17542 -.16960
  .02268 -.01426
 -.11862 -.13626 -.09637 -.30016 -.09221 -.05750 -.22113 -.02507 -.06444  .04961
  .00043  .10680 -.13295
 -.04653 -.18836 -.18436 -.24911 -.18642 -.17076 -.21014 -.18436 -.22113 -.03428
 -.20343 -.08964 -.16210 -.17542
 -.30016 -.27124 -.21602 -.35912 -.30945 -.36151 -.28175 -.25602 -.16418 -.11810
 -.25633 -.17542 -.39686 -.23478  .02987
  .03515
  .00805 -.01064
 -.40816 -.52754 -.46712
 -.32809 -.34486 -.39480 -.12656
                 ⋮
```

Since pre-processing (as described in Arabie and Soli's, 1982, Appendix) of Miller and Nicely's (1955) raw data (consisting of 17 matrices, each 16×16) led to symmetrized lowerhalf triangular matrices of confusions (similarities), IRDATA $= 1$ for the present analysis. (See list of other options below for IRDATA.) The next parameter, IPUNCH, controls punching on cards (or writing on a disk file) the final and certain intermediate values of $\mathbf{X}'$, the coordinates of the objects, and $\mathbf{W}'$, the weights of the sources, as well as other information (see options listed below). In the present analysis, IPUNCH $= -1$.

For most analyses, including this one, users will want to specify IPLOT $= 0$ (or just leave four blanks, which are treated as a zero), so as to get printer plots of all (pairwise) two-dimensional projections of the object spaces and (separately) of the source spaces. Thus, there will be $6(5)/2 = 15$ pages of plots for the six-dimensional object space and the same number for the corresponding source (weights) space, then $5(4)/2$ for each in the five-dimensional space, etc.

The fifth and final parameter on the second card, IRN, for determining the initial configuration of the objects in the MAXDIM-dimensional space (i.e., six-dimensional in the present analysis), is a topic discussed in some detail below. For the moment, let us note that the easiest option for the user is to specify a (positive) four-digit integer that serves as the "seed" for

SINDSCAL's self-contained random number generator. That generator provides the MAXDIM $\times I = 6 \times 16 = 96$ random numbers used as initial coordinates for the six-dimensional object space.

The third record in Table A.1 is a title card, the first 72 columns of which will appear frequently in the printed output from SINDSCAL. The fourth record is a single FORTRAN format card, which specifies for the program how the user has had each of the input proximity matrices punched on cards or entered as a file on disk. The format card of the data deck must have a left parenthesis in column one and should be constructed according to the rules for FORTRAN format statements, and any information beyond column 72 of that card will be ignored. (If necessary, a FORTRAN programmer or a FORTRAN manual should be consulted for assistance.) One should enter the data using such format conversion characters as E or F, which correspond to the floating point numbers, and avoid the format conversion for integer (namely I) even if the data are in fact integers.

The format statement is used once for each row of the data, and corresponds to exactly one row. The format should be sufficient to read in the entries of the card or record having the most data values (the number of entries in rows will vary for a triangular lowerhalf matrix), since no harm results if the format is not "used up" completely for shorter rows. If the longest row of the data matrix requires more than one card, the continuation cards for that row of the matrix should conform to the same format as the first card for that row. (If the final continuation card of the row is not completely used, no difficulties arise.) This arrangement works because the format is used over and over again if necessary, once for each card(s) of the row. The presence of a slash character, /, in the format often leads to trouble and should be avoided.

Then follows the first entry (for objects 2 and 1) of the first proximity matrix (corresponding to the "noise-masking condition" with S/N ratio of 12 dB, as listed in Table 2), and so on, until a blank record follows the last card, so that SINDSCAL terminates without expecting more data for another analysis.

SETTING UP CONTROL CARDS FOR SINDSCAL

The presentation of the parameter cards used for analyzing the Miller-Nicely (1955) data set (given above in Table A.1) lists the specific values of parameters used for that analysis but does not explain the alternative values potentially appropriate for other analyses. In this Appendix, we wish to list the various options and associated values. All the information given here is taken from Pruzansky's (1975) documentation for SINDSCAL, and readers are referred to that source for additional information. Table A.1 displays the positions of the various control parameters in the input deck, and we now wish to provide a more elaborate description of each than was given in the text.

First Parameter Card:

FORMAT: (4I4); VARIABLES: MAXDIM, MINDIM, NMAT, NSTIM

MAXDIM = maximum number of dimensions for solutions of the object space and (separately) the sources or weights space. This dimensionality cannot exceed 10.

MINDIM = minimum number of dimensions for same spaces just described; must be greater than or equal to 1.

NMAT = number of input proximity matrices (referred to as variable *K* in the text).

NSTIM = number of objects (referred to as *I* in the text).

Second Parameter Card:
FORMAT: (5I4); VARIABLES: ITMAX, IRDATA, IPUNCH, IPLOT, IRN

ITMAX = maximum number of iterations. When equal to zero, user must supply a "configuration deck" containing coordinates of the "constrained" object space, following immediately after the last input proximity matrix. This "configuration deck" for ITMAX = 0 provides *final* coordinates of the objects (i.e., as matrix $\mathbf{X}'$, the transpose of matrix $\mathbf{X}$, illustrated in Figure 3) from which the program is to provide (non-iterative) least squares estimates of the weights ($\mathbf{W}'$) as coordinates of the source space. When ITMAX exceeds zero, the program will proceed until either that number of iterations has been reached or until an internally specified lower limit on increase in variance accounted for (VAF) has been reached, and then terminate.

IRDATA specifies the form common to all *K* input proximity matrices.
= 1, similarities,
lower triangular halfmatrices without diagonals.
= 2, dissimilarities,
lower triangular halfmatrices without diagonals.
= 3, Euclidean distances,
lower triangular halfmatrices without diagonals.
= 4, product-moment correlations,
lower triangular halfmatrices without diagonals.
=−4, same as 4 but program normalizes each matrix so that sum of squares = 1.
= 5, covariances,
lower triangular halfmatrices with diagonals.
=−5, same as 5 but program normalizes each matrix so that sum of squares = 1.
= 6, similarities,
full *I* × *I* symmetric matrices (diagonal read but later ignored).
= 7, dissimilarities,
full *I* × *I* symmetric matrices (diagonal read but later ignored).

IPUNCH specifies the amount of intermediate and final results that will be punched as cards or written as a disk file, depending on job control language at the user's local computation center. All the options below *except* −1 include punching the "normalized solution," i.e., the matrices W' for the sources' weights and X' for the objects' coordinates. Note that options 1, 2, and 3 can lead to substantial quantities of output.

= −1, no punched output.
= 0, punch normalized solution only.
= 1, punch scalar products matrices.
= 2, punch three unnormalized matrices.
= 3, punch all of the above.

IPLOT is set to zero when all pairs of two-dimensional (i.e., planar) projections are to be printer-plotted for the object spaces and (separately) for the source spaces, for each dimensionality from MAXDIM to MINDIM. If IPLOT = −1, no plotting takes place. The user who wishes to use specialized plotting or other graphics capabilities at the local computer center should use the IPUNCH = 0 option listed above so that a file containing the matrices (W' and X') to be plotted will be accessible on disk to such equipment.

IRN determines how the initial configuration for X', objects' coordinates, is determined. A sufficient, but not necessary, condition for IRN = 0 is when ITMAX = 0, so that a user-supplied initial configuration *must* be supplied by the user. (This configuration will also constitute the *final* configuration. See further discussion in text on "constrained solutions.") When ITMAX ≠ 0, the user may still wish to specify that IRN = 0, so that an initial configuration for X' will be user-supplied and then iteratively refined and improved upon during the course of the program's ITMAX iterations.

Third and Fourth Parameter Cards:
These are respectively the title and FORTRAN FORMAT cards. See text and Table A.1 for details.

OPTIONAL CONFIGURATION FOR OBJECTS' COORDINATES

See headings above for ITMAX and IRN (both read in on the second parameter card), as well as Table A.1 and the text.

Blank Card:
If no further analysis is to follow, a blank record will terminate the run of SINDSCAL. If an additional analysis is to be run, begin immediately with a first control card just as if the next analysis had been the first to be performed.

APPENDIX B

The Carroll-Chang-Pruzansky Approach to Fitting the INDSCAL Model

In addition to proposing the INDSCAL model, Carroll and Chang (1970) also devised the first algorithm and associated computer program, also called INDSCAL (Chang and Carroll, 1969), for fitting this model. Pruzansky (1975) streamlined this program to produce a more efficient one called SINDSCAL. Subsequent to the earliest program, such other computer programs as ALSCAL (Takane, Young, and de Leeuw, 1977) MULTISCALE (Ramsay, 1977, 1978a, 1978b, 1980, 1981, 1982b, 1983) and N-NEWMDS (Okada and Imaizumi, 1980, 1986) were developed, using different algorithms and optimizing different criteria to fit the same INDSCAL model. Since the SINDSCAL program is the one for which the FORTRAN source code is most readily available and easily accessible, this Appendix (revised from Carroll and Wish, 1974b) will focus on the approach taken in SINDSCAL for fitting the INDSCAL model. (Readers interested in alternative algorithms should consult the references just cited.)

CONVERTING THE PROXIMITIES TO ESTIMATED DISTANCES

The first step, as in the "classical" metric two-way MDS procedure (see Kruskal and Wish, 1978, pp. 19-23), is to convert the *dissimilarities* to estimated distances. (If the input proximity data are similarities, they can be converted into dissimilarities, for example, by simply multiplying all values by -1.) The ensuing procedure is usually referred to as "estimation of the additive constant."

Under "metric" assumptions we may assume, without loss of generality, that

$$d_{ij,k} \cong \delta_{ij,k} + c_k . \qquad [B.1]$$

Dropping the (k) subscripts for the moment, the smallest constant c guaranteeing satisfaction of the *triangle inequality* $(d_{ij} \leqslant d_{i\ell} + d_{\ell j})$ for all triples (i, j, ℓ) can be given as

$$c_{\min} = \max_{(i,j,\ell)} (\delta_{ij} - \delta_{i\ell} - \delta_{\ell j}) . \qquad [B.2]$$

(Note: $c_{\min}$ *may* be negative.)

This approach to the "additive constant" estimation method for converting "comparative distances" (i.e., interval scale distance estimates) into absolute distances (i.e., ratio scale distance estimates), described in Torgerson (1958, pp. 276-277; also see Coxon, 1982, pp. 128-130) as the "one-dimensional subspace" scheme implicitly assumes that at least three points lie exactly on a straight line in the space. It is in many respects the simplest and most straightforward technique for additive constant estimation, and is the one used in the SINDSCAL program.

CONVERSION OF ESTIMATED DISTANCES TO ESTIMATED SCALAR PRODUCTS

If $\mathbf{x_i} = (x_{i1}, x_{i2}, \ldots, x_{iR})$ and $\mathbf{x_j} = (x_{j1}, x_{j2}, \ldots, x_{jR})$ are two vectors in R-dimensional space, their *scalar product*, usually written as $\mathbf{x_i} \cdot \mathbf{x_j}$ (which we shall also call b_{ij}) is defined as:

$$b_{ij} \equiv \mathbf{x_i} \cdot \mathbf{x_j} \equiv \sum_{r=1}^{R} x_{ir} x_{jr} \ . \qquad \text{[B.3]}$$

Geometrically, the scalar product can be interpreted as the cosine of the angle between the two vectors multiplied by the product of their lengths. Actually, however, this geometric fact is not really necessary for our purposes. Rather, it is quite sufficient to deal with the algebraic definition in equation [B.3].

In most applications of MDS, the *origin* of the space is not of any importance, and thus may be arbitrarily fixed because a shift in origin (defined by adding the same constant vector to all points' coordinates) leaves Euclidean distances unchanged. It has therefore become conventional to place the origin at the centroid, or generalized mean, of all the points.

While distances remain unchanged with a shift in origin, scalar products do not, since the vectors whose lengths and angles are involved are the vectors from the origin to the particular point. We can resolve this indeterminacy of scalar products, however, by always using scalar products from an origin at the centroid of all the points. We will henceforth assume that the origin is at the centroid, and will use the symbol b_{ij} to represent scalar products of vectors about such an origin.

As shown by Torgerson (1958), Euclidean distances may be converted by equation [B.4] into scalar products of vectors about an origin placed (arbitrarily) at the centroid of all the points:

$$b_{ij} = -\tfrac{1}{2}(d_{ij}^2 - d_{i.}^2 - d_{.j}^2 + d_{..}^2) \ , \qquad \text{[B.4]}$$

where

$$d_{i.}^2 = \frac{1}{I} \sum_j d_{ij}^2 \ , \qquad \text{[B.5]}$$

$$d_{.j}^2 = \frac{1}{I} \sum_i d_{ij}^2 \ , \qquad \text{[B.6]}$$

$$d_{..}^2 = \frac{1}{I^2} \sum_i \sum_j d_{ij}^2 \ . \qquad \text{[B.7]}$$

This conversion is equivalent to *doubly centering* the matrix of $-\frac{1}{2}$ times the *squared* interpoint distances (i.e., subtracting grand mean and row and column main effects, in the analysis of variance sense). A derivation of equation [B.4] follows.

Given

$$d_{ij}^2 = \sum_{r=1}^{R} (x_{ir} - x_{jr})^2 \ , \qquad \text{[B.8]}$$

assume

$$\sum_{i=1}^{I} x_{ir} = 0 \quad \text{for all } r = 1 \cdots R. \qquad [B.9]$$

(We may make that assumption without loss of generality, since the origin of the X space is arbitrary, and this procedure just fixes it at the centroid of all I points.) Expanding equation [B.8],

$$d_{ij}^2 = \sum_r (x_{ir}^2 - 2x_{ir}x_{jr} + x_{jr}^2)$$

$$= \sum_r x_{ir}^2 - 2\sum_r x_{ir}x_{jr} + \sum_r x_{jr}^2$$

$$= \ell_i^2 + \ell_j^2 - 2b_{ij} , \qquad [B.10]$$

where ℓ_i (used here because it is the first letter in "length," but bearing no relation to the subscript ℓ in equation [B.2]) is now defined as

$$\ell_i^2 \equiv \sum_r x_{ir}^2 , \qquad [B.11]$$

$$b_{ij} \equiv \sum_r x_{ir}x_{jr} \quad \text{(the scalar product).} \qquad [B.12]$$

Because of equation [B.9],

$$b_{i.} = b_{.j} = b_{..} = 0 , \qquad [B.13]$$

where the dot notation is analogous to that in equations [B.5] through [B.7], except that no term other than the denominator in [B.7] is now squared. From equations [B.10] and [B.13], we have

$$d_{i.}^2 = \ell_.^2 + \ell_i^2 , \qquad [B.14]$$

$$d_{.j}^2 = \ell_j^2 + \ell_.^2 , \qquad [B.15]$$

$$d_{..}^2 = 2\ell_.^2 , \qquad [B.16]$$

where

$$\ell_.^2 = \frac{1}{I} \sum_i \ell_i^2 . \qquad [B.17]$$

Then equations [B.10], [B.14], [B.15], and [B.16] together imply that

$$d_{ij}^2 - d_{i.}^2 - d_{.j}^2 + d_{..}^2 = -2b_{ij} . \qquad [B.18]$$

Multiplying both sides of equation [B.18] by $-\frac{1}{2}$ gives the desired result in equation [B.4].

At this point, the "classical" (two-way) metric MDS procedure à la Torgerson (1958) would simply *factor* this matrix $\hat{\mathbf{B}}$ into a product of the form

$$\hat{\mathbf{B}} \cong \hat{\mathbf{X}}\hat{\mathbf{X}}' \qquad [B.19]$$

to get estimates of the coordinates $\hat{x}_{ir}$. ($\hat{\mathbf{X}}$ is just the $I \times R$ matrix $\{\hat{x}_{ir}\}$ containing these estimated coordinates; matrix equation [B.19] is equivalent to the *scalar* equation $\hat{b}_{ij} \cong \sum \hat{x}_{ir}\hat{x}_{jr}$, the analogue of equation [B.3], but with estimates replacing exact values.)

This factorization usually is done by methods similar to principal components analysis (Hotelling, 1933) or factor analysis (Harman, 1976). Perhaps the best description was the procedure of Eckart and Young (1936), closely related to what is now referred to as the singular value decomposition (svd), for least squares approximation of an arbitrary matrix by a product of two matrices of smaller rank. When applied to a square symmetric matrix, such as $\hat{\mathbf{B}}$ presumably is (because $\hat{\mathbf{D}}^{(2)}$, the matrix of squared distance estimates, is square and symmetric), the Eckart-Young procedure results in two matrices (such as $\hat{\mathbf{X}}$ and $\hat{\mathbf{X}}'$) that are simply the transposes of one another. This statement is true as long as appropriate normalizing conventions are observed, and as long as the largest (in absolute value) R *eigenvalues* of $\hat{\mathbf{B}}$ are nonnegative, which is generally true in practice. Details of this procedure can be found in Torgerson (1958).

For readers familiar with the singular value decomposition of a matrix, the Eckart-Young analysis of $\hat{\mathbf{B}}$ is equivalent to approximating $\hat{\mathbf{B}}$ by the triple-product of (a) the matrix whose columns comprise the first R *left* singular vectors, (b) the diagonal matrix whose diagonals are the first R singular values, and (c) the matrix whose rows comprise the first R *right* singular vectors (all in corresponding order). Because of symmetry of $\mathbf{B}$, the singular values are the *absolute values of* the eigenvalues while the left and right singular vectors correspond to the eigenvectors of $\mathbf{B}$ (in the same order) with the same signs if the eigenvectors are nonnegative (and reversed signs in the case of negative eigenvectors). The practical import is that, if the first R eigenvalues are all nonnegative, they are identical to the first R singular values, while the first R left and right singular vectors are identical to each other, and to the first R eigenvectors. The Eckart-Young results establish, furthermore, that this particular R-dimensional decomposition yields the best rank R approximation, in an ordinary least squares sense, to $\hat{\mathbf{B}}$. Since (by assumption) the first R singular values are all positive (or at least nonnegative) their square roots are real numbers, and so the square root of each can be used to scale the corresponding eigenvector (singular vector) to produce the columns of $\mathbf{X}$.

In matrix notation, the full svd of $\hat{\mathbf{B}}$ is

$$\hat{\mathbf{B}} = \mathbf{U}\beta\mathbf{V}',$$

where $\mathbf{U}$ and $\mathbf{V}$ are $R \times R$ orthogonal matrices whose columns are left and right singular vectors of $\hat{\mathbf{B}}$, respectively, and β is a diagonal matrix containing the singular values. The restricted (R-dimensional) svd is given by:

$$\hat{\mathbf{B}} \cong \tilde{\mathbf{B}}_R = \mathbf{U}_R \beta_R \mathbf{V}_R' .$$

By the Eckart-Young results, $\tilde{\mathbf{B}}_R$ comprises the best R-dimensional least squares approximation to $\hat{\mathbf{B}}$. Because of the assumptions made above, the diagonal entries in β_R (i.e., the first R singular values) are all nonnegative, while $\mathbf{U}_R \equiv \mathbf{V}_R$. Therefore we may write this approximation (dropping the R subscripts on $\mathbf{U}$ and β) as

$$\hat{\mathbf{B}} \cong \mathbf{U}\beta\mathbf{U}' .$$

Since β has only nonnegative diagonals, $\beta^{1/2}$ exists (as a diagonal matrix with real values, namely the square roots of the nonnegative singular values), and we may define

$$\hat{\mathbf{X}} = \mathbf{U}\beta^{1/2} ,$$

in which case we have

$$\hat{\mathbf{B}} \cong \hat{\mathbf{X}}\hat{\mathbf{X}}' ,$$

so that $\hat{\mathbf{X}}$ as defined provides the best R-dimensional least squares approximation to the derived estimated scalar products matrix $\hat{\mathbf{B}}$.

THE INDSCAL MODEL IN SCALAR PRODUCT FORM

By applying the procedures described above (for converting estimated dissimilarities into estimated scalar products) to each two-way proximity matrix, we obtain a three-way array of estimated scalar products whose general entry is $b_{ij,k}$ (for source k and objects i and j). We now need to make an analogous conversion of the INDSCAL *model* into scalar product form.

By definition, the (true) scalar products for source k are defined as:

$$b_{ij,k} = \sum_r y_{ir,k} \, y_{jr,k} , \qquad [B.20]$$

where the $y_{ir,k}$ are defined as

$$y_{ir,k} = w_{kr}^{1/2} \, x_{ir} ,$$

that is, as the objects' coordinates in the "private" space for source k. Substituting this expression into equation [B.20], we have:

$$b_{ij,k} = \sum_r w_{kr} x_{ir} x_{jr} , \qquad [B.21]$$

which is the desired *scalar product form* of the INDSCAL model.

Equation [B.21] can easily be seen as a special case of what Carroll and Chang (1970) called the CANDECOMP (for CANonical DECOMPosition of N-way tables) model of the form (for $N = 3$):

$$z_{ij,k} = \sum_r a_{kr} b_{ir} c_{jr} . \qquad [B.22]$$

We get the INDSCAL model of equation [B.21] as a special case of the three-way CANDECOMP model of equation [B.22] by imposing the following constraints:

$$z_{ij,k} = b_{ij,k} \, , \qquad \text{[B.23]}$$

$$a_{kr} = w_{kr} \, , \qquad \text{[B.24]}$$

$$b_{ir} = c_{ir} = x_{ir} \, . \qquad \text{[B.25]}$$

For INDSCAL as a special case of this CANDECOMP (three-way) model we may, however, ignore the symmetry constraint of equation [B.25] and fit the model in its general form. Symmetry of the input proximities data is ordinarily sufficient to guarantee that (after appropriate normalization of the solution) b_{ir} will in fact equal c_{ir}.

AN ALGORITHM FOR FITTING THE CANDECOMP MODEL IN THE THREE-WAY CASE

Given the model

$$\hat{z}_{ij,k} \cong \sum_r a_{kr} b_{ir} c_{jr} \qquad \text{[B.26]}$$

(equation [B.22] with $\hat{z}_{ij,k}$ replacing $z_{ij,k}$ and $\cong$ replacing $\Rightarrow$) and "current estimates" of two sets of parameters (e.g., the b_{ir} values and c_{ir} values), we can find an exact least squares estimate of the third set by linear regression.

This result is obtained by reformulating the problem as

$$\hat{z}^{*}_{ks} \cong a_{kr} \hat{g}_{sr} \, , \qquad \text{[B.27]}$$

where

$$\hat{z}^{*}_{ks} = \hat{z}_{k(ij)} \qquad \text{[B.28]}$$

and

$$\hat{g}_{sr} = \hat{b}_{ir} \hat{c}_{jr} \qquad \text{[B.29]}$$

($\hat{b}_{ir}$ and $\hat{c}_{jr}$ are *current* estimates of b_{ir} and c_{jr}, respectively, and s is a subscript that is a function of i and j, and ranges over all values of i and j).

By this simple notational device, we have converted this original *trilinear* model into a *bilinear* model, which can be expressed in matrix notation as

$$\hat{Z}^{*} \cong A\hat{G}' \, . \qquad \text{[B.30]}$$

Note that the matrix $\hat{G}$ incorporates both the $\hat{b}$ values and $\hat{c}$ values, and the matrix A contains the a values. (Note that matrix G in this Appendix has no relation to the matrix of the same name in the text.) The $\cong$ implies that we seek the A providing the best least squares approximation to Z^{*}. This problem is a standard one, essentially equivalent to (least squares) multiple linear regression. In matrix notation, the least squares estimate of A is

$$\hat{A} = Z^{*}\hat{G}(\hat{G}'\hat{G})^{-1} \, . \qquad \text{[B.31]}$$

(This step in effect postmultiplies both sides of equation [B.30] by the right *pseudoinverse* of $\hat{G}'$.)

We use a general estimation scheme that Wold (1966) called a NILES (Nonlinear Iterative LEast Squares) procedure and that has since become known as alternating least squares (ALS) in the scaling (and more generally in the psychometric and statistical) literature. In the present case this approach requires iterating this least squares estimation procedure; i.e., estimating the a values (with b and c fixed) by least squares methods, then the b values (with a and c fixed) and so on round the iterative cycle until convergence occurs. In practice, the b and c values are set equal to each other during the final iteration of the alternating least squares procedure in SINDSCAL. While there is no guarantee that this process will converge to the *overall* least squares estimates of all three sets of parameters, it does seem to do so in most cases. There is a mild "local minimum" problem (tendency to converge to estimates such that no *small* change can improve the fit, although a *large* or global change can), but it seems to be minor. In practice the method seems "almost always" to converge to the global optimum solution. In any case the local minimum problem seems to be very slight in comparison with that in nonmetric two-way MDS, where the algorithms are generally based on a gradient or steepest descent method.

DIRECT SCALAR PRODUCTS DATA (CALLED "CORRELATIONS" OR "COVARIANCES") IN SINDSCAL

SINDSCAL allows the option (as did the older INDSCAL program of Chang and Carroll, 1969) of direct input of data interpreted as scalar products. Since such data are very frequently (but not necessarily) matrices of correlations or covariances derived from multivariate data, in the program these are called either "correlations" or "covariances". The difference, in practice, is that data called "correlations" are assumed to range between $+1$ and -1, and the diagonals are assumed to be equal to 1. Because of this last restriction, it is unnecessary to provide the diagonals, so the input can be a lower halfmatrix *without* diagonals. The SINDSCAL program simply fills in those missing diagonal entries with 1's in this case.

When the user declares that the data are "covariances," SINDSCAL requires from each source of data a lower halfmatrix with diagonal entries present. If the data are interpreted as "direct" judgments of scalar products but "self-proximities" are not available, the user must still estimate those entries when supplying the input, since the diagonals in a covariance matrix correspond to variances, which are generally not equal to one (as in a correlation matrix) or to each other. If the input data are product-moment correlations, they can still be declared "covariances" so long as the diagonal entries are included. When those diagonal entries are all unity (rather than, say, communality estimates), the result will be the same as providing only the lowerhalf matrix of correlations (without diagonals) and declaring the data as such.

The general rule on use of "scalar product" data as input to SINDSCAL is "if in doubt, call the data 'covariances,' but be sure in this case that diagonals are present".

APPENDIX C

The MULTISCALE II Procedure for Fitting the INDSCAL Model

Ramsay (1977, 1978a, 1978b, 1980, 1981, 1982b, 1983) proposed a maximum likelihood methodology for the MDS analysis of either two- or three-way proximities in his MULTISCALE approach. The former case uses $\{\delta_{ij,k}\}$, where the $k = 1 \cdots K$ sources are treated as replications. This approach implies either repeating the same task of data collection from a given source K times, or treating K different sources as homogeneous. In the three-way case, the proximity data are typically collected from K different sources, so that there is only a single "replication" for each. This Appendix briefly describes the approach taken in MULTISCALE II (the most recent version of MULTISCALE) to fitting the INDSCAL model.

Ramsay assumes that the $KI(I-1)/2$ observations $\delta_{ij,k}$ are independently and identically distributed with a probability density function given by $f\left(\delta_{ij,k} \mid d_{ij,k}, \sigma^2\right)$, where $d_{ij,k}$ represents the errorless weighted Euclidean distance between the two objects i and j for source k (equation [2] in the text), and σ is the standard error of a given input data value $\delta_{ij,k}$. Given this assumption of independence, the general form of the log likelihood function can be written as:

$$\log L = \sum_k \sum_{i<j} \log f\left(\delta_{ij,k} \mid d_{ij,k}, \sigma^2\right). \qquad [C.1]$$

The objective of this maximum likelihood formulation is to maximize [C.1] with respect to $\mathbf{X}$, $\mathbf{W}$, and the dispersion parameter σ^2.

Based upon arguments concerning the empirical behavior of the standard deviation of $\delta_{ij,k}$, Ramsay (1977, 1982b) advocates the use of the lognormal distribution for the density function f assumed in [C.1] so as to accommodate a constant ratio of standard deviation to mean for the untransformed input data. Thus,

$$f\left(\delta_{ij,k} \mid d_{ij,k}, \sigma^2\right) = (2\pi)^{-1/2}(\sigma\delta_{ij,k}) \exp\left[\frac{-\log^2\left(\delta_{ij,k}/d_{ij,k}\right)}{(2\sigma^2)}\right], \qquad [C.2]$$

which is equivalent to assuming that the logarithm of $\delta_{ij,k}$ has a normal distribution with a mean equal to $\log d_{ij,k}$ and a constant standard deviation σ^2. Thus, σ is invariant with respect to changes in the unit of measurement for proximities. (It is important to note that this distributional assumption requires the δ's to be measured on a *ratio* scale.)

Ramsay (1977, 1982b) estimates σ^2 independently of $\mathbf{X}$ and $\mathbf{W}$. He develops analytical expressions for σ^2 based on (a) a maximum likelihood estimate (MLE), (b) an asymptotically unbiased estimate, or (c) a Bayesian estimate. Assuming a uniform prior, all three estimates are equivalent up to a scale transformation since the denominators contain different terms, while the numerator is identical over the three. Define:

$$V = \sum_k \sum_{i<j} \log^2 \left[\frac{\delta_{ij,k}}{d_{ij,k}} \right];$$ [C.3]

then the log likelihood function exclusive of terms not containing parameters is:

$$\log L = -\frac{1}{2} \left[\frac{V}{\sigma^2} + M \log \sigma^2 \right],$$ [C.4]

where $M = KI(I-1)/2 =$ the total number of "independent" observations. From expression [C.4] above, the MLE for σ^2 is:

$$\hat{\sigma}^2 = \frac{V}{M}.$$ [C.5]

By substituting $\hat{\sigma}^2$ for σ^2 in [C.4], Ramsay (1977) forms the concentrated log likelihood function:

$$\log L = -\frac{M}{2} [\log V - 1 - \log M],$$ [C.6]

from which it follows that the maximum likelihood estimation of X and W is obtained by minimizing V, a badness-of-fit function for the lognormal distribution, with respect to X and W. However, because of the scalar indeterminacy problem between X and W in the INDSCAL model, as mentioned earlier in the text (under the section on the unique orientation of INDSCAL object spaces), Ramsay (1977) normalizes the weights so that the mean squared weight is one for each dimension. To impose this normalization, a Lagrangian approach to constrained optimization is used. The augmented log likelihood function to be maximized is:

$$Z = \log L - 1/2 \sum_r \lambda_r \left[\sum_k w_{kr}^2 - K \right],$$ [C.7]

where λ_r is the Lagrange multiplier for the r-th scaling constraint on the weights. Ramsay (1977) rearranges the gradients of Z to obtain implicit equations for X, W, and λ_r. Ramsay's (1982b) MULTISCALE II has a general procedure utilizing a scoring algorithm requiring first and second derivatives to estimate the desired set of parameters. The method of steepest ascent requiring only first derivatives can be utilized optionally. When the user imposes linear constraints on the object coordinates, a penalty function approach is adopted. Here, a penalty is subtracted from the log likelihood if the user-designated constraints are not satisfied. That is, this penalty has the value of zero if the constraints are exactly satisfied and is positive otherwise. Thus, in seeking the optimum in [C.7] of the difference between the log likelihood and penalty function, there will be a tendency toward attempting to satisfy the designated constraints. After the maximum of this expression is obtained, the penalty function is increased and the maximum is recomputed. This process is continued iteratively until the linear constraints are satisfied (cf. Fiacco and McCormick, 1968).

Because of the well-known asymptotic properties of maximum likelihood estimation, an asymptotic likelihood ratio test is available to test nested models. For example, one could test the hypothesis of competing dimensionalities of r and $r-1$ via:

$$Q = -2 \left(\log L_{r-1} - \log L_r\right), \qquad \text{[C.8]}$$

where $\log L_r$ is the log likelihood value for a fit in r dimensions. Here, Q has an asymptotic chi-square distribution with degrees of freedom equal to the difference in degrees of freedom for the two solutions. However, the test should not be taken very seriously in the three-way case unless each source's proximity data have been replicated, because the approximate chi-square statistic would be very far indeed from its asymptotic behavior, so that the chi-square distribution would approximate the actual distribution very poorly. Ramsay (1980) has, however, suggested some procedures for adjusting the degrees of freedom to improve the accuracy of this approximate distributional assumption.

APPENDIX D

The ALSCAL Procedure for Fitting the INDSCAL Model

Takane, Young, and de Leeuw (1977) have developed a general purpose computer program called ALSCAL that can accommodate a wide variety of different models and data. ALSCAL·4 (the most recent version of ALSCAL) can be utilized for either two-way (unweighted Euclidean) or three-way MDS (fitting either the INDSCAL or the IDIOSCAL model) to data that may (a) be defined on nominal, ordinal, interval, or ratio scales, (b) have missing observations, (c) be symmetric or nonsymmetric, (d) be treated as matrix conditional or matrix unconditional, (e) be replicated or unreplicated, and (f) be "continuous" or "discrete." The "continuous" versus "discrete" distinction, in the terminology used by Takane et al., concerns whether the "secondary" or "primary" (Kruskal, 1964) approach, respectively, to ties in monotone regression is used when the data are assumed to be ordinal scale. ALSCAL optimizes the fit of the model directly to the $\delta_{ij,k}$ by an alternating least squares procedure, unlike SINDSCAL which fits scalar products derived from the proximity data. We describe various technical aspects of ALSCAL in fitting the INDSCAL model to $\delta_{ij,k}$, for the case in which the data are assumed symmetric, ratio scale, matrix unconditional, and without missing data or replications.

ALSCAL's optimization problem for this case can be generally stated as attempting to estimate $\mathbf{X}$, $\mathbf{W}$, and the "disparity" array $\mathbf{D^*}$ to minimize a measure called SSTRESS, given as:

$$\text{SSTRESS} = \phi^2(\mathbf{X}, \mathbf{W}, \mathbf{D^*}) = \frac{\sum_k \sum_{i<j} \left[d_{ij,k}^{*2} - d_{ij,k}^2\right]^2}{[\text{A NORMALIZING FACTOR}]} \qquad \text{[D.1]}$$

where:

$$d_{ij,k}^2 = \sum_r w_{kr} (x_{ir} - x_{jr})^2, \qquad [D.2]$$

and

$$d_{ij,k}^{*2} = f[\delta_{ij,k}]. \qquad [D.3]$$

(The normalizing factor in the denominator of [D.1] will not be discussed further here; for details see Takane et al., 1977.)

The function $f[\cdot]$ in expression [D.3] is specified according to the scale of measurement declared for the input $\delta_{ij,k}$. The ALSCAL·4 algorithm involves four phases summarized as follows:

INITIALIZATION PHASE

This first stage generates starting estimates for **X**, **W**, and thus **D** by the Young, Takane, and Lewyckyj (1978) procedure involving first utilizing a singular value decomposition (svd) of an average derived scalar product matrix. The derivation of this matrix involves steps very similar but not identical to the pre-processing in SINDSCAL (see Appendix B) applied to each source matrix, followed by averaging over subjects. It differs primarily in the additive constant estimation scheme used, and also does not normalize the derived scalar products. The averaged scalar products matrix is then decomposed, using the svd, exactly as described in Appendix B for a single derived scalar product matrix in the "classical" Torgerson procedure for two-way MDS. Then a procedure similar to a method proposed by Schönemann (1972) for approximately fitting the INDSCAL model is used to find a rotation of the resulting configuration. This step is necessary since the use of the classical MDS analysis on the average derived (approximate) scalar product matrix yields a solution that is rotationally indeterminate. Details of the specific rotation scheme used can be found in Young et al. (1978).

OPTIMAL SCALING PHASE

Here, the intent is "optimal scaling" of the squared $\delta_{ij,k}$ observations to obtain the disparities $d_{ij,k}^{*2}$ which satisfy the selected measurement (scale) restrictions and are least squares estimates of the squared distances $d_{ij,k}^2$, given these measurement restrictions. That is, this phase maximizes the correlation between the observations and model's predictions, while respecting the measurement characteristics of $\delta_{ij,k}$. Thus, only the "optimal scaling" variables $d_{ij,k}^{*2}$ are estimated, while **X** and **W** are fixed, in order to minimize ϕ^2.

The first step in this phase is to compute $d_{ij,k}$, given current estimates of **X** and **W**. The second step entails performing the "optimal scaling." The *exact* nature of this operation depends upon the measurement assumptions concerning the scale type of $\delta_{ij,k}$. In general, all the various types of "optimal scaling" transformations can be defined as a linear transformation of the column vector **d** of $KI(I-1)/2$ components $d_{ij,k}^2$ ($i < j$) to obtain a second column vector **d***, containing the $KI(I-1)/2$ components $d_{ij,k}^{*2}$ ($i < j$)

$$\mathbf{d}^* = g(\mathbf{d}), \qquad [D.4]$$

where g is such a general linear transformation. Since **d*** is defined as a function of g, the SSTRESS minimand in expression [D.1] is minimized for fixed $\mathbf{W}$ and $\mathbf{X}$. In the matrix unconditional, ratio scale case, g can be represented via a projection operator $\mathbf{P}$ of the form:

$$\mathbf{P} = \boldsymbol{\delta}(\boldsymbol{\delta}'\boldsymbol{\delta})^{-1}\boldsymbol{\delta}', \qquad [D.5]$$

where $\boldsymbol{\delta}$ is the row vector containing the $KI(I-1)/2$ elements $\delta_{ij,k}^2$. In this case, the optimal scaling transformation involves estimating $\mathbf{d}^*$ via:

$$\mathbf{d}^* = \mathbf{Pd}. \qquad [D.6]$$

This step is equivalent to a very simple ordinary least squares linear regression (*without* a constant term) for a single independent variable ($\boldsymbol{\delta}$, as introduced in [D.5]) and a single dependent variable ($\mathbf{d}$).

In the case of the interval scale assumptions, the optimal scaling procedure is formally the same as in the ratio scale case, except there is one extra step; namely, the elements of $\boldsymbol{\delta}$ are not simply the squares of the original data values, but of those values plus an additive constant to be estimated (which varies for each source in the matrix conditional case, but is the same for all sources in the matrix unconditional case currently being considered), i.e., $\boldsymbol{\delta}$ contains values $\delta_{ij,k}^{*2} = (\delta_{ij,k} + c)^2$ where each c must be estimated by an optimal scaling criterion. Details of estimation of this additive constant can be found in Takane et al. (1977), with an important modification discussed in Young et al. (1978).

In the case of the more general measurement assumptions, the optimal scaling can be characterized formally using such a projection equation as in [D.6], but the projector $\mathbf{P}$ will, in these cases, be a function of both $\boldsymbol{\delta}$ and $\mathbf{d}$ and will be dependent on the scale type assumed, as well as whether the "continuous" or "discrete" option is assumed.

In practice, the optimal scaling for the ordinal and nominal cases is actually done by much more straightforward procedures. In the ordinal case, Kruskal's (1964) monotone regression algorithm is used, while in the nominal scale case the optimally scaled values are simply averages of d^2 values corresponding to the same value(s) of the nominal scale variable. The user can also specify starting values.

The final step of this phase involves normalizing the solution and the loss function (in order to prevent possible degenerate solutions). $\mathbf{X}$ is normalized so that the mean projection on each dimension is zero and the variance of the projections on each dimension is one. ALSCAL·4 also normalizes the "pseudoscalar" products from the optimally scaled data so that each source's sum of squared pseudoscalar products is one. According to Takane et al., this normalization (the same one used earlier in the SINDSCAL procedure, incidentally, and justified there analogously) facilitates the interpretation of source's sum of squared weights as an approximation of the VAF in the pseudoscalar products. Finally, the SSTRESS loss function is normalized for symmetric matrix unconditional data without missing entries to prevent the degenerate solution of $d_{ij,k}^2 = d_{ij,k}^{*2} = 0$ via

$$\phi_u^2 = \frac{\sum_k \sum_{i<j} \left[d_{ij,k}^{*2} - d_{ij,k}^2 \right]^2}{\sum_k \sum_{i<j} d_{ij,k}^{*4}}.$$ [D.7]

(As discussed earlier, other normalization options exist in cases of other types of data and/or analyses.)

TERMINATION PHASE

ALSCAL·4 terminates if the difference between successive pairs of computed SSTRESS values are acceptably close to zero.

MODEL ESTIMATION PHASE

Estimate W. The first subphase estimates W while holding X and D^* fixed. Define an $I(I-1)/2 \times R$ matrix S whose columns contain the components of the (unweighted) squared interpoint distances for each of the R dimensions, $(x_{ir} - x_{jr})^2$. Takane et al. (1977) also define a $K \times I(I-1)/2$ matrix $\overline{D}^*$, whose rows contain the $I(I-1)/2$ "optimally scaled" observations for each source. We can now rewrite the unnormalized stress minimand in expression [D.1] as:

$$\phi^2(S, W, \overline{D}^*) = tr(\overline{D}^* - WS')'(\overline{D}^* - WS'),$$ [D.8]

where tr denotes the trace of a matrix, and the conditionally optimal estimate of W is:

$$\hat{W} = \overline{D}^* S(S'S)^{-1}.$$ [D.9]

Naturally, there is no explicit constraint that $w_{kr} \geqslant 0$ using expression [D.8]. However, ALSCAL·4 does permit optional nonnegativity constraints on the w_{kr}.

Estimation Procedure for X. ALSCAL·4 utilizes an implicit equation procedure to obtain a new conditional least squares estimate for each coordinate x_{ir} of a single object i for dimension r ($r = 1 \cdots R$). This estimation phase retains D^* and W at their current (fixed) values. The partial derivative of the normalized SSTRESS loss function in expression [D.7] with respect to x_{ir} can be expressed using one unknown: x_{ir} (cf. Schiffman, Reynolds, and Young, 1981). The resulting expression with one unknown is then set equal to zero and the value of x_{ir} is solved for by standard techniques. All the other coordinates except x_{ir} are fixed at their current values while x_{ir} is being estimated. Immediately upon solving for this new value of x_{ir}, its previous value is updated, and the procedure then estimates the new value of another coordinate. ALSCAL·4 thus successively obtains values for each coordinate of object i, one at a time, replacing the previous values with the newly estimated ones. This procedure continues for object i until the estimates stabilize. ALSCAL·4 then shifts to another object and continues until new coordinates for all objects are estimated. Once this procedure is completed for all objects, ALSCAL·4 returns to the "optimal scaling" phase.

REFERENCES

Akaike, H. (1974). A new look at the statistical model identification. *IEEE Transactions on Automatic Control, 19*, 716-723.

Arabie, P. (1973). Concerning Monte Carol evaluations of nonmetric scaling algorithms. *Psychometrika, 38*, 607-608.

Arabie, P. (1978a). Random versus rational strategies for initial configurations in nonmetric multidimensional scaling. *Psychometrika, 43*, 111-113.

Arabie, P. (1978b). The difference between "several" and "single": A reply to Spence and Young. *Psychometrika, 43*, 119.

Arabie, P., & Carroll, J. D. (1980a). *How to use MAPCLUS, a computer program for fitting the ADCLUS model.* Unpublished manuscript, AT&T Bell Laboratories (Room 2F-128A), Murray Hill, NJ.

Arabie, P., & Carroll, J. D. (1980b). MAPCLUS: A mathematical programming approach to fitting the ADCLUS model. *Psychometrika, 45*, 211-235.

Arabie, P., & Carroll, J. D. (1987). Conceptions of overlap in social structure. In L. Freeman, D. R. White, & A. K. Romney (Eds.), *Research methods of social network analysis.* Farifax, VA: George Mason University Press.

Arabie, P., Carroll, J. D., DeSarbo, W. S., & Wind, J. (1981). Overlapping clustering: A new method for product positioning. *Journal of Marketing Research, 18*, 310-317.

Arabie, P., & Shepard, R. N. (1973, August). *Representation of similarities as additive combinations of discrete, overlapping properties.* Paper presented at Mathematical Psychology Meetings, Montréal.

Arabie, P., & Soli, S. D. (1982). The interface between the types of regression and methods of collecting proximity data. In R. G. Golledge & J. N. Rayner (Eds.), *Proximity and preference: Problems in the multidimensional analysis of large data sets* (pp. 90-115). Minneapolis, MN: University of Minnesota Press.

Asimov, D. (1985). The grand tour: A tool for viewing multidimensional data. *SIAM Journal on Scientific and Statistical Computing, 6*, 128-143.

Baker, F. B., & Hubert, L. J. (1976). A graph-theoretic approach to goodness-of-fit in complete-link hierarchical clustering. *Journal of the American Statistical Association, 71*, 870-878.

Bentler, P. M., & Lee, S.-Y. (1978). Statistical aspects of a three-mode factor analysis model. *Psychometrika, 43*, 343-352.

Bentler, P. M., & Lee, S.-Y. (1979). A statistical development of three-mode factor analysis. *British Journal of Mathematical and Statistical Psychology, 32*, 87-104.

Bieber, S. L. (1986). A hierarchical approach to multigroup factorial invariance. *Journal of Classification, 3*, 113-134.

Bisanz, G. L., LaPorte, R. E., Vesonder, G. T., & Voss, J. F. (1978). On the representation of prose: New dimensions. *Journal of Verbal Learning and Verbal Behavior, 17*, 337-357.

Bisanz, G. L., & Voss, J. F. (1982, June). *Developmental changes in understanding story themes: Scaling and process analyses.* Paper presented at meeting of the Canadian Psychological Association, Montréal, Canada.

Bloxom, B. (1968). Individual differences in multidimensional scaling. *Research Bulletin 68-45.* Princeton, NJ: Educational Testing Service.

Bloxom, B. (1978). Constrained multidimensional scaling in *N* spaces. *Psychometrika, 43*, 397-408.

Bloxom, B. (1984). Tucker's three-mode factor analysis model. In H. G. Law, C. W. Snyder, Jr., J. A. Hattie, & R. P. McDonald (Eds.), *Research methods for multimode data analysis.* (pp. 104-121). New York: Praeger.

Brady, H. E. (1985). Statistical consistency and hypothesis testing for nonmetric multidimensional scaling. *Psychometrika, 50*, 509-537.

Carroll, J. D. (1968). *A justification of D-squared as a second-order proximity measure.* Unpublished manuscript, AT&T Bell Laboratories, Murray Hill, NJ.

Carroll, J. D. (1975, August). *Models for individual differences in similarities.* Paper presented at Eighth Annual Mathematical Psychology Meeting, Purdue University, West Lafayette, IN.

Carroll, J. D. (1985). [Review of *Multidimensional Scaling*]. *Psychometrika, 50*, 133-140.

Carroll, J. D. (1986). *The interpretation of weights in the INDSCAL model.* Unpublished manuscript, AT&T Bell Laboratories, Murray Hill, NJ.

Carroll, J. D., & Arabie, P. (1979, June). *INDCLUS: A three-way approach to clustering*. Paper presented at Meeting of the Psychometric Society, Monterey, CA.

Carroll, J. D., & Arabie, P. (1980). Multidimensional scaling. In M. R. Rosenzweig & L. W. Porter (Eds.), *Annual review of psychology* (Vol. 31, pp. 607-649). Palo Alto, CA: Annual Reviews.

Carroll, J. D., & Arabie, P. (1982). *How to use INDCLUS, a computer program for fitting the individual differences generalization of the ADCLUS model*. Unpublished manuscript, AT&T Bell Laboratories (Room 2F-128A), Murray Hill, NJ.

Carroll, J. D., & Arabie, P. (1983). INDCLUS: An individual differences generalization of the ADCLUS model and the MAPCLUS algorithm. *Psychometrika, 48*, 157-169.

Carroll, J. D., & Chang, J. J. (1970). Analysis of individual differences in multidimensional scaling via an *N*-way generalization of "Eckart-Young" decomposition. *Psychometrika, 35*, 283-319.

Carroll, J. D., & Chang, J. J. (1972, March). *IDIOSCAL (Individual Differences in Orientation SCALing): A generalization of INDSCAL allowing IDIOsyncratic reference systems as well as an analytic approximation to INDSCAL*. Paper presented at meeting of the Psychometric Society, Princeton.

Carroll, J. D., Clark, L. A., & DeSarbo, W. S. (1984). The representation of three-way proximity data by single and multiple tree structure models. *Journal of Classification, 1*, 25-74.

Carroll, J. D., & Wish, M. (1974a). Models and methods for three-way multidimensional scaling. In D. H. Krantz, R. C. Atkinson, R. D. Luce, & P. Suppes (Eds.), *Contemporary developments in mathematical psychology: Vol. 2. Measurement, psychophysics, and neural information processing* (pp. 57-105). San Francisco: Freeman.

Carroll, J. D., & Wish, M. (1974b). Multidimensional perceptual models and measurement methods. In E. C. Carterette & M. P. Friedman (Eds.), *Handbook of perception: Vol. 2. Psychophysical judgment and measurement* (pp. 391-447). New York: Academic Press.

Chang, J. J., & Carroll, J. D. (1968). *How to use PROFIT, a computer program for property fitting by optimizing nonlinear or linear correlation*. Unpublished manuscript, Murray Hill, NJ: AT&T Bell Laboratories.

Chang, J. J., & Carroll, J. D. (1969). *How to use INDSCAL, a computer program for canonical decomposition of N-way tables and individual differences in multidimensional scaling*. Unpublished manuscript, AT&T Bell Laboratories, Murray Hill, NJ.

Chang, J. J., & Carroll, J. D. (1980). Three are not enough: An INDSCAL analysis suggesting that color space has seven (±1) dimensions. *Color Research and Application, 5*, 193-206.

Chang, W. C. (1983). On using principal components before separating a mixture of two multivariate normal distributions. *Applied Statistics, 32*, 267-275.

Coombs, C. H. (1964). *A theory of data*. New York: Wiley.

Corter, J., & Tversky, A. (1986). Extended similarity trees. *Psychometrika, 51*, 429-451.

Coxon, A. P. M. (1982). *The user's guide to multidimensional scaling*. Exeter, NH: Heinemann.

Coxon, A. P. M., & Jones, C. L. (1977). Multidimensional scaling. In C. A. O'Muircheartaigh & C. Payne (Eds.), *The analysis of survey data: Vol. 1. Exploring data structures* (pp. 159-182). New York: Wiley.

Coxon, A. P. M., & Jones, C. L. (1978). *The images of occupational prestige*. New York: St. Martin's.

Coxon, A. P. M., & Jones, C. L. (1979a). *Class and hierarchy: The social meaning of occupations*. New York: St. Martin's.

Coxon, A. P. M., & Jones, C. L. (1979b). *Measurement and meanings*. New York: St. Martin's.

Cronbach, L. J., & Gleser, G. C. (1953). Assessing similarity between profiles. *Psychological Bulletin, 50*, 456-473.

de Leeuw, J., & Heiser, W. (1982). Theory of multidimensional scaling. In P. R. Krishnaiah & L. N. Kanal (Eds.), *Handbook of statistics: Vol. 2. Classification, pattern recognition and reduction of dimensionality* (pp. 285-316). Amsterdam: North-Holland.

DeSarbo, W. S. (1982). GENNCLUS: New models for general nonhierarchical clustering analysis. *Psychometrika, 47*, 449-475.

DeSarbo, W. S., & Carroll, J. D. (1985). Three-way metric unfolding via alternating weighted least squares. *Psychometrika, 50*, 275-300.

DeSarbo, W. S., & Rao, V. R. (1984). GENFOLD2: A set of models and algorithms for the GENeral unFOLDing analysis of preference/dominance data. *Journal of Classification, 1*, 147-186.

86

Eckart, C., & Young, G. (1936). The approximation of one matrix by another of lower rank. *Psychometrika, 1*, 211-218.

Eckes, T. (1981). *Formale Modelle zu Ähnlichkeitsstrukturen.* Doctoral Dissertion, University of the Saar. Saarbrücken, West Germany.

Eckes, T. (1981/1982). Zwei diskrete Modelle zu Ähnlichkeitsstrukturen im Vergleich: Das hierarchische und das additive Cluster-Modell. *Archiv für Psychologie, 134*, 281-302.

Efron, B. (1982). *The jackknife, the bootstrap and other resampling plans.* Philadelphia: SIAM (Society for Industrial and Applied Mathematics).

Ekman, G. (1963). A direct method for multidimensional ratio scaling. *Psychometrika, 28*, 33-41.

Fiacco, A. V., & McCormick, G. P. (1968). *Nonlinear programming: Sequential unconstrained minimization techniques.* New York: Wiley.

Gill, P. E., & Murray, W. (1974). Newton-type methods for unconstrained and linearly constrained optimization. *Mathematical Programming, 28*, 311-350.

Green, P. E., & Rao, V. R. (1972). *Applied multidimensional scaling: A comparison of approaches and algorithms.* New York: Holt, Rinehart and Winston.

Hahn, J., Widaman, K. F., & MacCallum, R. (1978, August). *Robustness of INDSCAL and ALSCAL with respect to violations of metric assumptions.* Paper presented at meeting of the Psychometric Society, Hamilton, Ontario, Canada.

Harman, H. H. (1976). *Modern factor analysis* (3rd ed.). Chicago: University of Chicago Press.

Harshman, R. A. (1970). Foundations of the PARAFAC procedure: Models and conditions for an "explanatory" multi-modal factor analysis. *UCLA Working Papers in Phonetics, 16*, 1-84.

Harshman, R. A. (1972a). Determination and proof of minimum uniqueness conditions for PARAFAC 1. University of California at Los Angeles, *Working Papers in Phonetics 22.*

Harshman, R. A. (1972b). PARAFAC2: Mathematical and technical notes. University of California at Los Angeles, *Working Papers in Phonetics 22.*

Harshman, R. A., & Lundy, M. E. (1984). The PARAFAC model for three-way factor analysis and multidimensional scaling. In H. G. Law, C. W. Snyder, Jr., J. A. Hattie, & R. P. McDonald (Eds.), *Research methods for multimode data analysis* (pp. 122-215). New York: Praeger.

Hartigan, J. A. (1967). Representation of similarity matrices by trees. *Journal of the American Statistical Association, 62*, 1140-1158.

Hartigan, J. A. (1975). *Clustering algorithms.* New York: Wiley.

Holman, E. W. (1972). The relation between hierarchical and Euclidean models of psychological distances. *Psychometrika, 37*, 417-423.

Horan, C. B. (1969). Multidimensional scaling: Combining observations when individuals have different perceptual structures. *Psychometrika, 34*, 139-165.

Hotelling, H. (1933). Analysis of a complex of statistical variables into principal components. *Journal of Education Psychology, 24*, 499-520.

Hubert, L. (1972). Some extensions of Johnson's hierarchical clustering algorithms. *Psychometrika, 37*, 261-274.

Hubert, L. J. (1974). Some applications of graph theory to clustering. *Psychometrika, 39*, 283-309.

Hubert, L. J., Golledge, R. G., Constanza, C. M., Gale, N., & Halperin, W. C. (1984). Nonparametric tests for directional data. In G. Bahrenberg, M. M. Fischer, & P. Nijkamp (Eds.), *Recent developments in spatial data analysis* (pp. 171-189). Aldershot, England: Gower.

Jardine, C. J., Jardine, N., & Sibson, R., (1967). The structure and construction of taxonomic hierarchies. *Mathematical Biosciences, 1*, 173-179.

Johnson, S. C. (1967). Hierarchical clustering schemes. *Psychometrika, 32*, 241-254.

Jones, C. L. (1983). A note on the use of directional statistics in weighted Euclidean distances multidimensional scaling models. *Psychometrika, 48*, 473-476.

Jones, L. E., & Dong, H.-K. (1980, May). *Multidimensional scaling of original and derived dissimilarities when the underlying dimensions are of differential salience.* Paper presented at the meeting of the Psychometric Society, Iowa City, IA.

Kim, J.-O., & Mueller, C. W. (1978). *Factor analysis: Statistical methods and practical issues.* Newbury Park, CA: Sage.

Knoke, D. (1983). Organization sponsorship and influence: Representation of social influence associations: *Social Forces, 61*, 1065-1087.

Kroonenberg, P. M. (1983). *Three-mode principal component analysis: Theory and applications.* Leiden, The Netherlands: DSWO Press.

Kroonenberg, P. M., & de Leeuw, J. (1980). Principal component analysis of three-mode data by means of alternating least squares algorithms. *Psychometrika, 45*, 69-97.

Kroonenberg, P. M., Lammers, C. J., & Stoop, I. (1985). Three-mode principal component analysis of multivariate longitudinal organizational data. *Sociological Methods and Research, 14*, 99-136.

Kruskal, J. B. (1964). Nonmetric multidimensional scaling: A numerical method. *Psychometrika, 29*, 115-129.

Kruskal, J. B. (1977). The relationship between multidimensional scaling and clustering. In J. Van Ryzin (Ed.), *Classification and clustering* (pp. 19-44). New York: Academic Press.

Kruskal, J. B., & Wish, M. (1978). *Multidimensional scaling*. Newbury Park, CA: Sage.

LaPorte, R. E., & Voss, J. F. (1979). Prose representation: A multidimensional scaling approach. *Multivariate Behavioral Research, 14*, 39-56.

Law, H. G., Snyder, C. W., Jr., Hattie, J. A., & McDonald, R. P. (1984). *Research methods for multimode data analysis*. New York: Praeger.

Ling, R. F. (1971). Cluster analysis. Ann Arbor, MI: University Microfilms. No. 71-22356.

Lundy, M. E., & Harshman, R. A. (1985). *Reference manual for PARAFAC analysis*. London, Ontario: Scientific Software Associates.

MacCallum, R. C. (1977). Effects of conditionality on INDSCAL and ALSCAL weights. *Psychometrika, 42*, 297-305.

Meulman, J., Heiser, W., & Carroll, J. D. (1987). *How to use PREFMAP3*. Unpublished manuscript, AT&T Bell Laboratories (Room 2F-128A), Murray Hill, NJ.

Miller, G. A. (1969). A psychological method to investigate verbal concepts. *Journal of Mathematical Psychology, 6*, 169-191.

Miller, G. A., & Nicely, P. E. (1955). An analysis of perceptual confusions among some English consonants. *Journal of the Acoustical Society of America, 27*, 338-352.

Miller, K., & Gelman, R. (1983). The child's representation of number: A multidimensional scaling analysis. *Child Development, 54*, 1470-1479.

Miller, R. G. (1974). The jackknife — a review. *Biometrika, 61*, 1-15.

Murtagh, F. (1985). *Multidimensional clustering algorithms*. Vienna: Physica-Verlag.

Namboodiri, K. (1984). *Matrix algebra*. Newbury Park, CA: Sage.

Nygren, T. E., & Jones, L. E. (1977). Individual differences in perceptions and preferences for political candidates. *Journal of Experimental Social Psychology, 13*, 182-197.

Okada, A., & Imaizumi, T. (1980). Nonmetric method for extended INDSCAL model. *Behaviormetrika, 7*, 13-22.

Okada, A., & Imaizumi, T. (1986). How to use nonmetric Euclidean/non-Euclidean weighted multidimensional scaling program (N-NEWMDS Version 1.1). *Journal of Applied Sociology, 27*, 1-81.

Pruzansky, S. (1975). *How to use SINDSCAL: A computer program for individual differences in multidimensional scaling*. Unpublished manuscript, AT&T Bell Laboratories (Room 2F-128A), Murray Hill, NJ.

Purcell, A. T. (1984). Multivariate models and the attributes of the experience of the built environment. *Environment and Planning B: Planning and Design, 11*, 193-212.

Rabin, M. D., & Frank, M. (1982). Unpublished work, University of Connecticut Health Center, Farmington.

Ramsay, J. O. (1975). Solving implicit equations in psychometric data analysis. *Psychometrika, 40*, 337-360.

Ramsay, J. O. (1977). Maximum likelihood estimation in multidimensional scaling. *Psychometrika, 42*, 241-266.

Ramsay, J. O. (1978a). Confidence regions for multidimensional scaling analysis. *Psychometrika, 43*, 145-160.

Ramsay, J. O. (1978b). *MULTISCALE: Four programs for multidimensional scaling by the method of maximum likelihood*. Chicago: National Educational Resources, Inc.

Ramsay, J. O. (1980). Some small sample results for maximum likelihood estimation in multidimensional scaling. *Psychometrika, 45*, 139-144.

Ramsay, J. O. (1981). MULTISCALE. In S. S. Schiffman, M. L. Reynolds, & F. W. Young (Eds.), *Introduction to multidimensional scaling: Theory, method, and applications* (pp. 389-405). New York: Academic Press.

Ramsay, J. O. (1982a). Some statistical approaches to multidimensional scaling data. [With discussion.] *Journal of the Royal Statistical Society A, 145*, 285-312.

Ramsay, J. O. (1982b). *MULTISCALE II manual*. Mooresville, IN: International Education Services.

Ramsay, J. O. (1983). MULTISCALE: A multidimensional scaling program. *American Statistician, 37*, 326-327.

Rosenberg, S. (1977). New approaches to the analysis of personal constructs in person perception. In J. K. Cole (Ed.), *Nebraska Symposium on Motivation* (Vol. 24, pp. 179-242). Lincoln: University of Nebraska Press.

Rosenberg, S. (1982). The method of sorting in multivariate research with applications selected from cognitive psychology and person perception. In N. Hirschberg & L. G. Humphreys (Eds.), *Multivariate applications in the social sciences* (pp. 117-142). Hillsdale, NJ: Erlbaum.

Rosenberg, S., & Kim, M. P. (1975). The method of sorting as a data-gathering procedure in multivariate research. *Multivariate Behavioral Research, 10*, 489-502.

Schiffman, S. S., Reynolds, M. L., & Young, F. W. (1981). *Introduction to multidimensional scaling*. New York: Academic Press.

Schönemann, P. H. (1972). An algebraic solution for a class of subjective metrics models. *Psychometrika, 37*, 441-451.

Schwartz, G. (1978). Estimating the dimension of a model. *Annals of Statistics, 6*, 461-464.

Shepard, R. N. (1972a). A taxonomy of some principal types of data and of multidimensional methods for their analysis. In R. N. Shepard, A. K. Romney, & S. B. Nerlove (Eds.), *Multidimensional scaling: Theory and applications in the behavioral sciences. Vol. 1. Theory* (pp. 21-47). New York: Seminar Press.

Shepard, R. N. (1972b). Psychological representation of speech sounds. In E. E. David, Jr., and P. B. Denes (Eds.), *Human communication: A unified view* (pp. 67-123). New York: McGraw-Hill.

Shepard, R. N. (1974). Representation of structure in similarity data: Problems and prospects. *Psychometrika, 39*, 373-421.

Shepard, R. N. (1980). Multidimensional scaling, tree-fitting, and clustering. *Science, 210*, 390-398.

Shepard, R. N. (1987). George Miller's data and the birth of methods for representing cognitive structures. In W. Hirst (Ed.), *Giving birth to cognitive science: A Festschrift for George A. Miller*. New York: Cambridge University Press.

Shepard, R. N., & Arabie, P. (1979). Additive clustering: Representation of similarities as combinations of discrete overlapping properties. *Psychological Review, 86*, 87-123.

Shoben, E. J., & Ross, B. H. (in press). Cognitive psychology and multidimensional scaling. In R. R. Ronning, J. Glover, J. C. Conoley, & J. Witt (Eds.), *The influence of cognitive psychology on testing* (pp. 229-266). Hillsdale, NJ: Erlbaum.

Soli, S. D., & Arabie, P. (1979). Auditory versus phonetic accounts of observed confusions between consonant phonemes. *Journal of the Acoustical Society of America, 66*, 46-59.

Soli, S. D., Arabie, P., & Carroll, J. D. (1986). Representation of discrete structure underlying observed confusions between consonant phonemes. *Journal of the Acoustical Society of America, 79*, 826-837.

Srivastava, R. K., Alpert, M. I., & Shocker, A. D. (1984). A customer-oriented approach for determining market structures. *Journal of Marketing, 48*, 32-45.

Stevens, S. S. (1951). Mathematics, measurement, and psychophysics. In S. S. Stevens (Ed.), *Handbook of experimental psychology* (pp. 2-49). New York: Wiley.

Takane, Y., Young, F. W., de Leeuw, J. (1977). Nonmetric individual differences multidimensional scaling: An alternating least squares method with optimal scaling features. *Psychometrika, 42*, 7-67.

Takane, Y., Young, F. W., & Lewyckyj, R. (1978). Three notes on ALSCAL. *Psychometrika, 43*, 433-435.

Torgerson, W. S. (1958). *Theory and methods of scaling*. New York: Wiley.

Tucker, L. R (1964). The extension of factor analysis to three-dimensional matrices. In N. Frederiksen & H. Gulliksen (Eds.), *Contributions to mathematical psychology*, (pp. 109-127). New York: Holt, Rinehart and Winston.

Tucker, L. R (1972). Relations between multidimensional scaling and three-mode factor analysis. *Psychometrika, 37*, 3-27.

Tucker, L. R, & Messick, S. J. (1963). An individual differences model for multidimensional scaling. *Psychometrika, 38*, 333-368.

Tukey, J. W. (1958). Bias and confidence in not-quite so large samples (Abstract). *Annals of Mathematical Statistics, 29*, 614.

Tversky, A. (1977). Features of similarity. *Psychological Review, 84*, 327-352.

Weinberg, S. L., & Carroll, J. D. (1986, June). *Choosing the dimensionality of an INDSCAL-derived space by using a method of resampling.* Paper presented at the meeting of the Classification Society of North America, Columbus, Ohio.

Weinberg, S. L., Carroll, J. D., & Cohen, H. S. (1984). Confidence regions for INDSCAL using the jackknife and bootstrap techniques. *Psychometrika, 49*, 475-491.

Wish, M. (1969, October). *Individual differences in perceived dissimilarity among stress patterns of English words.* Paper presented at Psychonomic Society Meeting, St. Louis.

Wish, M. (1976). Comparisons among multidimensional structures of interpersonal relations. *Multivariate Behavioral Research, 11*, 297-324.

Wish, M., & Carroll, J. D. (1974). Applications of individual differences scaling to studies of human perception and judgment. In E. C. Carterette & M. P. Friedman (Eds.), *Handbook of perception: Vol. 2. Psychophysical judgment and measurement* (pp. 449-491). New York: Academic Press.

Wish, M., & Kaplan, S. J. (1977). Toward an implicit theory of interpersonal communication. *Sociometry, 40*, 234-246.

Wold, H. (1966). Estimation of principal components and related models by iterative least squares. In P. R. Krishnaiah (Ed.), *Multivariate analysis* (pp. 391-420). New York: Academic Press.

Young, F. W. (1984). The general Euclidean model. In H. G. Law, C. W. Snyder, Jr., J. A. Hattie, & R. P. McDonald (Eds.), *Research methods for multimode data analysis* (pp. 440-469). New York: Praeger.

Young, F. W., & Lewyckyj, R. (1981). *ALSCAL-4 users guide.* Unpublished manuscript, University of North Carolina. L. L. Thurstone Psychometric Laboratory, Chapel Hill.

Young, F. W., & Null, C. H. (1978). Multidimensional scaling of nominal data: The recovery of metric information with ALSCAL. *Psychometrika, 43*, 367-379.

Young, F. W., Takane, Y., & Lewyckyj, R. (1978). Three notes on ALSCAL. *Psychometrika, 43*, 433-435.

ABOUT THE AUTHORS

PHIPPS ARABIE is Professor of Psychology and Sociology at the University of Illinois at Champaign and has also been Visiting Professor of Computer Science at University College Dublin. His research interests include multidimensional scaling, clustering and other forms of combinatorial data analysis, models of judgment, and social networks. Funding for this research has been provided by several programs of the National Science Foundation, the Mathematics Program of the Office of Naval Research, the National Institute of Justice, and AT&T Information Systems. He is the Founding Editor of the *Journal of Classification* and also serves on the Editorial Boards of *Journal of Applied Psychology* and *Sociological Methods and Research*, as well as the Advisory Committee of *Connections*. He is also the author of numerous articles in scholarly journals and books.

J. DOUGLAS CARROLL is a Distinguished Member of Technical Staff at AT&T Bell Laboratories, where he does research on multidimensional scaling and related techniques as a member of the Information Principles Research Laboratory. He has taught at Yale, N.Y.U., C.U.N.Y., the University of California at San Diego and at Irvine, and the University of Pennsylvania. He is an Associate Editor of *Psychometrika*, on the Editorial Board of the *Journal of Classification*, and Consulting Editor for the *Journal of Experimental Psychology: General*, is past president of the Psychometric Society, the Classification Society and the Society of Multivariate Experimental Psychology, as well as a Fellow of the American Psychological Association, the American Statistical Association, and AAAS. He has published widely in such journals as *Psychometrika, Journal of Classification, Journal of Mathematical Psychology*, and *Journal of Marketing Research*, as well as in a number of books and other publications.

WAYNE S. DeSARBO is the Howard and Judy Berkowitz Chair Associate Professor of Marketing at the Wharton School of the University of Pennsylvania, and was formerly a member of Technical Staff in the Mathematics and Statistics Research Center at Bell Laboratories in Murray Hill, NJ. He received his B.S. degree in Economics from the Wharton School of the University of Pennsylvania in 1971 and has M.A. degrees in

Sociology, Administrative Science, and Marketing from Yale University and the University of Pennsylvania. He obtained his Ph.D. in Marketing and Statistics from the University of Pennsylvania in 1978, and completed post doctorate work in Operations Research and Econometrics there. He has published over 50 articles in such journals as *Journal of Marketing Research, Journal of Consumer Research, Psychometrika, Decision Science, Journal of Classification,* and *Marketing Science.* His research interests involve the development of new quantitative methodologies for the further understanding of product positioning, market segmentation, and consumer choice.

NOTES

NOTES

NOTES

Quantitative Applications in the Social Sciences

(a Sage University Papers Series)

$6.00 each

SAGE PUBLICATIONS, INC.
P.O. BOX 5084
NEWBURY PARK, CALIFORNIA 91359—9924

Place
Stamp
here